LUCY CALKINS AND NATALIE LOUIS

Writing for Readers: Teaching Skills and Strategies

DEDICATION

To Randy and Katherine Bomer, who understand that the teaching Natalie and others like her do is our best hope for democracy.

WITHDRAWN

FirstHand
An imprint of Heinemann
A division of Reed Elsevier Inc.
361 Hanover Street
Portsmouth, NH 03801-3912
www.heinemann.com

Offices and agents throughout the world

TOURO COLLEGE LIBRARY
Kings Hwy

Photography: Peter Cunningham

Rubrics and checklists adapted by permission from *New Standards*. The *New Standards*® assessment system includes performance standards with performance descriptions, student work samples and commentaries, on-demand examinations, and a portfolio system. For more information, contact the National Center on Education and the Economy, 202-783-3668 or www.ncee.org.

Library of Congress Cataloging-in-Publication Data

Calkins, Lucy McCormick.
    Writing for readers : teaching skills and strategies / Lucy Calkins and Natalie Louis.
    p. cm. — (Units of study for primary writing ; 3)
    ISBN 0-325-00530-3 (pbk. : alk. paper)
    1. English language-Composition and exercises-Study and teaching (Primary)—United States. 2. Readability (Literary style)—Study and teaching (Primary) 3. Curriculum planning-United States. I. Louis, Natalie. II. Title.
    LB1529.U5C358 2003
    372.62'3--dc22   2003019532

ISBN 0-325-00530-3

Printed in the United States of America on acid-free paper

07   06   05   ML   4   5

SERIES COMPONENTS

▶ **The Nuts and Bolts of Teaching Writing** provides a comprehensive overview of the processes and structures of the primary writing workshop.

▶ You'll use **The Conferring Handbook** as you work with individual students to identify and address specific writing issues.

▶ The seven **Units of Study**, each covering approximately four weeks of instruction, give you the strategies, lesson plans, and tools you'll need to teach writing to your students in powerful, lasting ways. Presented sequentially, the Units take your children from oral and pictorial story telling, through emergent and into fluent writing.

▶ To support your writing program, the **Resources for Primary Writers CD-ROM** provides video and print resources. You'll find clips of the authors teaching some of the lessons, booklists, supplementary material, **reproducibles** and **overheads**.

PART FIVE: **Preparing for Publication**

WRITING FOR READERS: TEACHING SKILLS AND STRATEGIES

This study begins with us, as teachers, confessing to our children that we have a hard time reading their writing. Prior to now, we've reveled in children's approximations. Now, it's as if we let the cat out of the bag. "I took your wonderful stories home last night," we say, "and I sat down to read them. But do you know what . . . I read a bit and then I got stuck. I couldn't figure out what the story was supposed to say! Has that ever happened to any of you?"

Until now, we've so wanted our children to feel good as writers that we have hidden our struggles to translate their spindly letters into meaning. When neither we or the child could decipher a text, we have tended to distract the child from this state of affairs by turning quickly to the picture or to the next story . . . anything to avoid this child confronting the sad fact that, alas, the work of his or her hands isn't readable. The problem with this is that the only reason children will care about spelling, punctuation, or white space is that these conventions make it easier for others to read and to appreciate their texts! It's *crucial*, therefore, that as soon as a child has the ability to begin to write in ways a reader could conceivably read, we let him or her in on the truth.

Why This Unit?

If children are going to approach spelling and punctuation with the same resourcefulness, verve, and energy that they bring to the rest of the writing curriculum, we must approach the teaching of conventions with equal resourcefulness, verve, and energy. Our goal in this unit is to spotlight the importance of spelling and punctuation by designing a unit of study that makes word walls, blends, and capital letters into the talk of the town. We know, of course, that it will take far more than a month for children to grow strong in their abilities to write conventionally, but we also know that there can be great benefits to shining a curricular spotlight on the critical importance of conventions.

When young children work at spelling the words of their lives, they engage in the most hands-on, active, challenging form of graphophonics work imaginable. A child who wants to spell *umbrella* or *spaghetti* or *thunderstorm* will break the child labor laws, putting himself through a far more demanding regimen than a teacher could ever assign. And in writing workshops, young writers not only initiate this work, they also persist at it with awesome tenacity. Those of us who teach young writers can't let this learning opportunity go by unnoticed.

About the Unit

The unit of study, however, can't stand alone. It relies upon teachers explicitly teaching phonics and high-frequency words during word-study time and through interactive writing and shared reading. Specifically, we teach children to bring their knowledge of letters, sounds, and high-frequency words into both the reading and writing workshops. This study can make a world of difference. It's potent, powerful stuff; but the study can backfire if you're not careful.

The risk is that this unit could scare your children away from being active, resourceful spellers and lead them to retreat into a hyper-concern for convention. The last thing you want is for teaching to make your children passive and dependent, lining up behind you for correct spellings. The last thing you want is for your children to settle for "The dog bit at me," instead of writing "The dog snarled at me," because of a concern for correctness! It's also conceivable that this unit could frighten children into regarding writing as an opportunity to display their control of conventions more than as an opportunity to convey meaning.

It's especially wise, therefore, to do some assessment before you enter this unit. Before you embark, be confident that your children see writing as a way to make and communicate meaning, and that they regard the writing workshop as a place to share their own important stories. They must be able to generate ideas for writing and to write (or tell) stories that stretch across several pages. They should be fearless (if not skilled!) spellers. That is, before embarking on this unit, you hope that the child who wants to write about a *bulldozer* will have the courage and confidence to tackle the word *bulldozer* even if he hears only a very few sounds. Before this study, then, you hope your children are driven by a desire to tell their stories and that this matters enough so that they won't sacrifice their wonderful content when you nudge them to write more conventionally.

Then, too, you'll want to look at your children's command of conventions and judge whether, after a solid month of work, *almost all* your children will be able to write *rbt* for *rabbit*, *sn* for *sun*, and *hoz* for *house*. That is, your hope is that by the middle of this unit, when your children ask themselves, "Can I read this?" the answer can be at least a tentative "Yes."

If all the hard work in the world will still result in the answer to "Can you read this?" being "No way," then you'll want to postpone this unit by a month. For example, we postponed the study in some urban kindergartens where many children, in November, still had sound-letter correspondence for only a tiny handful of letters. In these classrooms, we tended to create a detour study, designed to bring children along so that by December, they would be ready for this study. In some of the detour studies children wrote labels, and in others they wrote list-books.

Either way, we decreased the volume of the writing they were expected to do, and increased expectations for conventional-ness. I summarize a detour study in Chapter 3 (Planning Curriculum in a Primary Writing Workshop) of the first book in the series, *The Nuts and Bolts of Teaching Writing*.

Although we added a detour study in some kindergartens, for the majority of our kindergarten classrooms and for almost all our first and second grades, we were clear that children would profit from this unit if it were scheduled for late autumn.

This book chronicles the story of one month in Natalie Louis' teaching. Natalie's low-income school had four ability-grouped first-grade classes, and Natalie's was the lowest of these. Half of the students came from Spanish-speaking homes and didn't speak fluent English. Natalie's class held eight children with special education needs.

At the start of the year, less than half of Natalie's first graders passed the first rung of an assessment in which (in a one-to-one conversation with Natalie), they were asked to attach either a letter name or a sound to any alphabet letter, to point to first the front and then the back of a book, and then show where on a page they would start reading. Most of Natalie's children did not know the meaning of stop signs, red-ring-with-slash "no" signs, or pictorial signs indicating girls' and boys' bathrooms.

During the year in which this book was written, Natalie made countless minor yet crucial adjustments so that the writing workshop would flourish amidst the challenges of her class. Though it didn't start this way, the routine in Room 103 became that while her children were still wearing their coats and carrying their book bags, they sat at their assigned places. Only after a child was seated did Natalie give that child a pencil, another greeting, and a "Do Now" sheet that asked the child to circle pictures that began with a particular sound or do a page of handwriting practice. While Natalie's children were anchored to their seats with these less-than-ideal "Do Now" papers, she sent children to the coat rack a few at a time, connected personally with individuals, and tried to ease the most dramatic tensions so that soon her children would be ready for morning meeting. Every teacher will need to make adjustments in response to his or her students' needs to make writing workshop work well for his or her own class.

Natalie usually does five or ten minutes of interactive writing during her morning meetings, and I describe that interactive writing in *The Nuts and Bolts of Teaching Writing* and on the CD-ROM. Always, Natalie reads aloud and does some shared reading as part of morning meeting. Her children may join together in song. Then it's time for the writing workshop. Natalie regards the writing workshop as the time in her day when her children make their most progress as readers as well as writers.

INSPIRING CHILDREN TO WRITE FOR READERS

GETTING READY

▶ Invented-spelling story on a chart paper booklet with the first two pages readable and the final page indecipherable— make it a cliff-hanger.

▶ Supply of stapled-together booklets of three to four pieces of paper as at the end of the previous unit. Renew the supply every day.

▶ Children disengaged from partners from last unit. Perhaps you'll assign new rug spots; in any case you must disengage preexisting partnerships so that you can later initiate new partnerships (see Session X).

▶ Each child's set of past pieces of writing—some readable, some not. You'll bring these old pieces out in Session II, but be sure you have them now.

⊙ See CD-ROM for resources

DURING THIS UNIT, YOUR TEACHING WILL FOCUS *on the conventions of print, but your children, meanwhile, will also carry on with the writing processes they learned in prior units. That is, they'll need to work with some independence to choose topics, plan their writing, and to record small moments of their lives. You'll establish the context for the new work children will tackle in this study by conveying that for the next few weeks, your children will continue choosing topics and writing true stories.*

Although most of the explicit teaching in this unit expands children's knowledge of print, children also need to spend time each day rehearsing for and writing stories. It is crucial that all children, especially children such as those in Natalie's class, have time and opportunities to mess about with story language and story structure. They need to learn that in stories, one thing happens and then the next and the next, and they need to internalize transitions such as then *or* finally. *For some children, one of the great challenges of school is that they are required to use language not only to communicate messages but also to build a world and to re-create life in that world—to tell real stories. Although this unit doesn't explicitly teach storytelling, it is enormously important that children continue to have opportunities to use all they have learned so far this year.*

In this first session, you will aim to convey the big picture of this new unit. Specifically, you'll inspire children to work harder and in new ways so that others can read their writing.

The Minilesson

Connection

Tell students that in the new unit, their Tiny Moment stories will get even better.

"Do you remember how on Friday we celebrated our Tiny Moment stories? Do you remember how proud you were of your work? Well, today, we are going to continue to write Tiny Moment stories. And we are going to begin a new unit that will help us make our Tiny Moment stories even better."

Teaching

Tell a detailed story of trying to read your children's writing. Help your children feel your great yearning to read their stories and your frustrations when you couldn't.

"I need to tell you about something that happened to me Friday night. Okay? Ready? Well, on Friday, right after our Tiny Moments celebration, I brought all your writing home with me. (I couldn't bear to leave it in school!) And so Friday night I started watching TV and then I said, 'Wait a minute. Why am I watching TV when I have my kids' stories at home?' I thought, 'My kids' stories would be so much better than this show!' So I turned off the TV and I got the box of your writing, and some tea, and a blanket, and I wrapped myself up and snuggled down to read, like this." Natalie reenacted the utter bliss of the moment and showed how she reached for a story. "I started to read." Turning to the first page of the dummy chart-sized book, Natalie pointed at the words and read, "Me and my sister went on the ropes."

ME ND MI SITER WNT ON DA ROPS

Still acting the part of her Friday-night-reading self, Natalie said, "Oh, I can't wait to see what happens next!" Turning the page, she read, "We climbed the bumps. We went high."

Notice that Natalie refers to focused vignettes as Tiny Moments. In the previous book, Abby referred to these as Small Moments. Classrooms, like families, develop a private shared language. Invent your own language in your classroom, using some phrases over and over. Notice also that this "connection" is atypical. Natalie does not end by naming exactly what she will teach today.

Natalie is wise to couch this reading narrative into the "Friday night at my house" setting, making it a memorable and concrete anecdote. Sometimes when we talk to young children about reading and writing we become highly abstract and metacognitive, talking about in-the-brain strategies in ways that children can't always grasp. The concrete detail of Natalie's story provides a welcome alternative.

Take the time to paint a scene, to recreate the image of you, snuggling down to read your children's work. Your longing to read what your children have written will become the force behind this whole unit. This is not window dressing, it's crucial! Play up your involvement in the first section of this story so that your children empathize when you encounter difficulties and can't read on.

WE CIMD DA BMPS WE WNT HI

Turning to the final page, Natalie looked at the print and then stopped in her tracks. She looked very confused:

WIGSDNR DADHSDN.

"Wait a minute! What happened next?" she said and peered at the page. "Oh my gosh!" Turning back through the pages, she reread and retold the cliff-hanger of a story, this time letting her intonation show the rising suspense. "They were on the rope. They had climbed up the bumps, the knots, and they were high. And . . . And . . . I'm left hanging!"

Now stepping back out of the role play, Natalie said to her class, "I had to stop reading this great story without learning how it ended because I couldn't read it." She speaks with woe. "I was so sad that the writer hadn't written in a way that let me read the whole story." Today, I want us to realize that it can be a really sad thing to not be able to read a story, and that's true if it's our own story or someone else's story."

Active Engagement

Tell the children to turn and talk to a friend about what made the last page harder to read than the first two. Listen in to and coach these conversations.

"Could you turn to a friend and tell your friend what made that last page so difficult to read?"

Alain and Sebastien, twin brothers, turned to talk. Alain said, "That last page has some crazy writing! Sebastien, look at it! I think I write like that sometimes. With some crazy stuff."

Sebastien nodded, "Yeah, I think you write crazy."

Listening in, Natalie interjected, "Boys, I know you think that writing is crazy, but could you talk to each other about *why* it is crazy?"

Notice that Natalie's example of readable prose isn't perfectly spelled. She isn't setting the goal too high for her children, and the work is carefully chosen to inspire, not demoralize. Notice also that the story is a brief Small Moment story. Natalie isn't addressing the nature of this text in her minilesson, but her story, nevertheless, functions as a model. And her teaching is cumulative, building on the preceding unit of study.

Imagine every child in the class turning to talk with his or her friend, and Natalie and I crouching among the pairs of children, listening in on their conversations. Very often we draw from what we hear in these partnership conversations to cite one example of the sort of thing we hope children are saying. We do not have the whole class report on what they said to each other!

Alain looked at the page, "Well, it's all smushed together. You can't have all of those letters smushed up like that."

Sebastien agreed, "Yeah, I think so too."

Link

Urge the children to write so that readers can read their writing. Ask them to remember that you'll be sitting at home, hoping to read all of the pages of their better-than-TV stories.

"As you go off to write today and for the next few weeks, try really hard to keep me in your mind. I want you to remember that I am at home, dying to get to the end of your amazing stories, and I am hoping that your writing has given me the help I need to get to the end. Your writing is so, so much better than TV . . . and I can't bear to have to stop halfway through it."

Alain and Sebastien say that letters can't be all scrunched up, but they still have a difficult time un-scrunching letters in their own writing. When a child doesn't have white space between words, it's not necessarily enough to tell the child, "Add white spaces." The problem may be that the child doesn't yet have a strong concept of what a word is.

Eventually, of course, you will ask your children to keep a broader range of readers in mind—but for now, the easiest-to-grasp and most tangible goal you can give your children is for them to write in a way that you can read their stories. This will be an appealing goal because your children no doubt adore you and long to please you. Eventually, you'll encourage children to reread their own writing and to write also for their peers, but don't mention these audiences now. Let that come in time. . . .

Obviously, Natalie knows that simply telling her children to write for readers isn't going to do the job . . . but it's a start.

TIME TO CONFER

Look for children who know that their writing is not as readable as it could be. Celebrate this awareness. Your goal will be for them to want to write so that others can read it, and to be willing to work toward this goal. So yes, you are asking them to look at the writing and to say, with some sadness, "I bet NO ONE can read this!" Your goal will be to transform discouragement into resolve to do more to help readers. Be ready to celebrate and name any productive activity a child takes toward the goal of writing for readers. In most of your conferences over the next few days, you will help the writer hear and record a sound, and then the next sound . . . The differences between conferences will be in how they start rather than in what you accomplish. Sometimes the beginning will be the child's recognition (or yours) that the writing is an illegible string of letters (see "Let Me Help You Put Some Words Down"). Sometimes, it will be a child's nervousness to write unknown words. Sometimes it will be a child who is stymied by a difficult word. In any case, you will coach the child to isolate a sound, find and record letters to match it, then to reread, and to articulate the word again, to hear the next sound. . . . The last thing you want is for children to become so intent on spelling well that they compromise their content. This means you'll also continue to hold conferences such as those in your last unit of study. Although most of your conferences in this session will help writers record sounds, your real message will be that writers plan out great stories . . . and then use letter-sound knowledge to write in ways others can read.

This conference in *The Conferring Handbook* may be especially helpful today:

▶ *"Say and Record a Word, Then Reread"*

Also, if you have *Conferring with Primary Writers*, you may want to refer to the following conference:

▶ "Let Me Help You Put Some Words Down"

After-the-Workshop Share

Tell the children about a writer who did something to make his or her writing more readable. In this instance, Juliser has reread her own writing often in the midst of writing.

"Hey everyone, today Juliser did the coolest thing. Juliser finished writing the first page of her story, and she realized that she could not read what she had written. She remembered that I would be reading her story while I'm home alone tonight, without her. She knew she had to do *something* so I could understand her story. So she started over. She crossed out what she'd written and this time, after she wrote a little bit, *she reread her own writing*. Then she wrote some more and *then* she *reread her writing again* like this. Let me show you how she did this."

(Natalie had made an enlarged copy of the start of Juliser's story on chart paper.) Stepping into the role of Juliser, Natalie put her finger under the letters and reenacted Juliser reading the words she had written and articulating what she wanted to write next "Me *and*." Now Natalie wrote *and*, and went back to reread "Me and." Soon she'd voiced "mommy" and had written her approximation of that.

"I bet a lot of you found ways to make sure that when I'm at home tonight, I won't get totally stuck trying to read your stories. How many of you wrote in ways that will help me read your writing?" Across the room, children signified that yes, indeed, they'd done this. "I'll be taking them home tonight and I can't wait to read them."

Notice that Natalie retells what Juliser did in a way that recollects the main lesson from the day and that makes Juliser look like she worked with independence, without relying on Natalie. The true story could have been said this way, "I helped Juliser to use a strategy . . ." but Natalie wisely downplays her own role in the account, saying instead, "Juliser decided to. . . ."

Notice that Natalie doesn't just talk about what Juliser did. She reenacts it. That is, instead of giving an explanation, she gives a demonstration. The demonstration is deliberately tailored to highlight the one thing Natalie wants to emphasize, which is the process Juliser went through as she voiced the word she wanted to write, isolated a sound, recorded it, reread, and then voiced it again.

IF CHILDREN NEED MORE TIME

In Session II you will journey over the same terrain as this session and will do so in a similar way. For this reason, there is no advantage to lingering with this session. Remember also that your goal for this session isn't to equip your children with the skills necessary to write for readers. Instead, your goal is to help children yearn to write in such a way that you can read their writing. If all that your children learn in this session is that they want to write for you as their first reader, this alone would be a grand accomplishment. You can't expect miracles.

After school, lay out this first day's writing. Make two piles: the easy-to-read writing, and the not-so-easy-to-read writing. Take the not-so-easy-to-read pile and try to identify why each of these pieces is difficult to read. What common trouble spots does your class have?

For the next workshop, you'll need to set aside four to six pieces from each child's work, starting at the beginning of the year. Now is a good time to look at the growth you can and cannot see from the first piece to today.

Natalie's children's writing at the start of this unit might not look great, but when we set her children's work at the start of this unit against the backdrop of their writing histories, we were struck by how much growth had taken place. You will be able to see growth in your children, too, as you look back at their writing. You need to notice what your children *can do*.

Sebastien began the year writing scrawls, then progressed to labeled drawings. Now, he had written a sentence on each page of a two-page booklet. His writing looked at first glance as if it was random strings of letters [*Fig. I-1*] but in fact, a close look showed that Sebastien was actually representing most of the consonant sounds in words. (See the translations.)

Shavon's word choice sparkled with originality (I walked in the park. My mom brought my brother bitsy boy.) but it, too, could easily have been pushed aside as nothing more than a random string of letters. [*Fig. I-2*]:

IWINThPOCMIMBUTMIdrrBBUY

We decided to keep each child's first few samples of writing from early in the year in his or her folder throughout this unit as a tangible reminder to us *and to the child* of the journey that child had traveled.

Fig. I-1   Sebastien

I was going to my cousin's house.
I was playing snowboards.

Fig. I-2   Shavon

I walked in the park. My mom brought my
brother bitsy boy.

EXAMINING READABLE AND UNREADABLE WRITING

GETTING READY

- An enlarged, hard-to-read line or two of writing. You'll probably want to write this on your own, pretending it's a child's.
- Each child's writing folder with work from early in the year (the "hard-to-read" examples) and last session's writing (the more readable examples).
- Writing paper and utensils, as always.
- See CD-ROM for resources

LAST NIGHT YOU READ THROUGH *what your children had done as they worked with new resolve to write in ways that you could read. Today, you probably have a million things in your mind that you could teach. You probably have a long list in your mind of all the things your children are not able to do. With any luck, you wrote that list down somewhere. That's good. Now, remember to focus on what your kids can do on their own. You are going to need that can-do list today to teach them how to take the next step. Remember to begin with what each child knows. Starting with what each child doesn't know can make you feel overwhelmed. It can sap your energy before you even begin to teach. Remember, in this journey toward more conventional writing, as in all journeys, each person can only move forward one step, then another, then another.*

In this session you will ask the children to divide their writing into piles— one of readable and one of virtually unreadable writing. You are trying to hand over the awareness of what makes texts readable; you want children to have readers in mind as they write. The children will share why some texts were in the unreadable pile and will collect thoughts about what's necessary for writing to be readable.

THE MINILESSON

Connection

Remind children that in the last session, they wrote so that you could read it. Tell them that today, _they'll_ try to read their writing, dividing it into piles as they go.

"Everyone, I had the most fun night last night! I took your writing home, and I read the work you did yesterday in class, and I could see that most of you tried really hard to make it easier for me to read your stories. For the next few weeks, we are _all_ going to work extra hard to make our writing easier to read. Remember how yesterday, Juliser asked me, 'Can you read this?' Today what I want you to know is that _I'm not the only one_ who'll be trying to read your writing. _You_ will be trying to read your stories too. We'll ask that question—'Can you read this?' to _ourselves_ as well as to me."

Teaching

Teach children how to work hard at reading their writing by demonstrating how you, as a reader, go about trying to read one of their stories.

"So let's try it. Today we're going to try _really hard_ to read our own writing. If it is pretty easy to do, we'll put it in one pile, and if it's hard to do, we'll put it in the hard pile. This takes a special kind of hard-work reading. I want you to watch what I did at home last night when I really, really, REALLY wanted to read your writing. Pretend I'm at home, and I have a wonderful stack of your stories right here. Watch—this is what I did."

Natalie got one child's writing and looked at it. She didn't show the piece to the class but did hold it in her lap and then visibly pulled closer to peer at it. "Oh yeah, that shows Shawn on his bike," she said, pointing at part of the picture. "I don't know who this person in the picture is, but it _might_ be Anthony, his brother."

This is an artful connection. Natalie recalls yesterday's work in a way that sets children up for today's work. She makes today into a small step forward from yesterday. Even the wording she uses to describe yesterday is parallel to that which she uses to describe today. Notice also the specificity with which she recalls Juliser's writing—details in the minilessons always teach more than generalizations.

Notice how the plan for this minilesson, like so many others, builds upon the one that went before it. It is often true that one-third of a minilesson is repetitive and two-thirds is new.

Natalie sets children up by telling them what she hopes they notice. Then she role-plays how she reads hard-to-read writing. She speculates over what the picture probably shows. While she teaches this work in the writing workshop, she is, of course, teaching similar lessons in the reading workshop. Using illustrations as a source of knowledge is as important to readers of published children's literature as it is to readers of children's own stories.

Pausing, she said to the class, "Think in your mind what I just did."

Show children that you point under the print and use problem-solving strategies when you encounter difficulty reading hard-to-read texts.

Continuing, Natalie said to herself, "Let me try to read the words. I copied them up on the easel." As she said this, Natalie displayed the enlarged writing on the easel, and put her finger under the first word. "'I rd.' Hmm. What could that say? 'I rd (?)'" She read on. "'my bike?' Oh! I got it. 'I rode my bike.'" Natalie reread to be sure, 'I rode my bike,' and gestured to the drawing, saying, "Yep, that matches."

Ask the class to name the strategies they saw you using.

Then, turning to the group, Natalie asked, "What did you notice me doing when I *really* wanted to read Robert's story?" The group agreed that Natalie had used the picture and all she knew about Robert to help, and that she'd pointed under the words and read with an "I bet I can figure this out" attitude. Most of all, she hadn't given up easily.

"I can read this writing! I'm going to put it in the 'readable' pile over here. If I get one that I can't read, even when I try as hard as I just tried, then I'm going to put it in my 'unreadable' pile over on this other side."

Active Engagement

Ask the children to read through the writing in their own folders and make two piles, the more- and less-readable writing.

"Right now, will each of you open your folder and reread the writing that is in it. Remember to do your best, hard-work-reading. As you reread your writing, make two piles, like I did—one for the readable writing, and one for the writing you just can't read very well."

"If you come to pieces that have no words or that you can't read, don't feel bad or embarrassed, just put those pieces in the pile of hard-to-read writing. This is no time to feel bad. We're at the very start of our unit and soon we'll *all*

Natalie is nudging children to be active even at the very start of her demonstration. She hasn't done much yet—just pulled close to study the illustration—but she already asks kids to articulate for themselves what she just did. She intervenes to be sure her kids are processing her demonstration.

The secret is to act like you are six and to role-play the strategic work you'd do (and the work you hope your children will do). Although you want to act in strategic, problem-solving ways, don't persevere too long. Today your children will be ready to learn from the gist of what they see; that is, they'll learn from the fact that you're working hard to read writing, not from any of your specific strategies.

Here, Natalie, asks kids to articulate what they noticed her doing as part of the teaching, not the active engagement component, of the minilesson. She could instead have made this into the active engagement component. When we do that, however, instead of practicing or trying out what we have taught (as Natalie's children do soon) children merely talk about what they have seen. The active engagement is most helpful if children practice the actual work they will be doing, instead of merely talking about the work.

Ideally, you will have doctored up the folders so each contains just four or six pieces, some hard-to-read ones from very early in the year and at least one or two easier-to-read pieces from more recently.

It is really important to address the emotional aspects of this unit. You are wise to tell children they mustn't feel badly when some writing needs to go in the hard-to-read pile.

write so people can read our writing. Your hard-to-read writing pile is a good thing right now because it will teach you all kinds of important stuff."

As the children sorted their writing, Natalie and I circulated, listening and coaching.

Ask the children to share their piles with a friend, talking together about *why* one pile is hard to read and the other is easier.

"Now that you have sorted your writing into two piles, talk to a friend about what makes the hard-to-read writing so hard to read, and what makes the easier pile easier. Tell your friend *why* some is hard and some is easy to read. Be ready to share this with the whole group in a minute or two." Soon animated conversations were under way. Not surprisingly, the children didn't necessarily talk about what makes the hard-to-read writing a challenge, but instead talked about their abilities to write conventionally.

Daniel announced to Lilly, "I only have one pile. Ms. Louis said we need two piles. I don't have no writing 'easy-to-read' pile."

Lilly shrugged. "So? Ms. Louis isn't mad. I got two piles. I am almost the same as you, with one pile, but I got one story my mom did with me at home. It was easy 'cause my mom spelled the words."

This seemed like a good idea to Daniel, who said, "My dad is good at words, like your mom. I can make my writing good too."

Meanwhile, Natalie (who'd not been mad at all about Daniel's one pile) was beginning to get worried. "Everyone, I heard what you were saying about how your parents can be good helpers. That's *one* way you could make your writing easier to read—by asking someone to spell the words for you. I am glad your parents are good at writing words, and I like that they want to help you, but if your parents help you too much, then you won't be practicing. During this unit, you kids are going to learn to help yourselves. That way, when your mom and dad and I are not here, you can still write stories people can read. I know every one of you wants to learn to help yourselves."

Notice we ask children to talk to a friend rather than to their partners. This is because we disbanded the formal partnerships so that we can reinstitute them with some drumroll later on in the unit. While children talk among themselves, we eavesdrop on this conversation so that we can learn how they understand our teaching.

When you get a glimpse of trouble, it's usually wise to assume there is more trouble, hidden from your eyes. Address it. Don't avert your eyes and hope it goes away.

You'll find yourself acting as part-preacher, part-teacher during this unit. Don't stop talking up the values you want to promote in your children. They need you to talk up courage and perseverance and resolve—because all this and much more is asked of them.

Signal for the class to come back together. Generate a short list of features that make some writing easier to read.

"Okay everyone, will you stop what you are saying? That was so cool! I loved watching you work so hard to read your own writing. All of you are like I am when I have a story. You *really* wanted to read your stories just like I really want to read them! Sometimes you realized you couldn't figure out WHAT you wrote. That's okay. We're just at the start of the unit. Now, can you say out loud what you found out about why some writing is easier to read than other writing? I'll write your ideas down so we can remember them. Tell us why some of your writing was hard to read, and what made other pieces in the other pile easier to read."

This was the list Natalie and the children made that day:

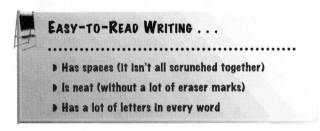

EASY-TO-READ WRITING . . .

▸ Has spaces (it isn't all scrunched together)
▸ Is neat (without a lot of eraser marks)
▸ Has a lot of letters in every word

Link

Refer back to the list of why some writing is hard to read and some, easy. Remind your writers to try making their writing easy to read in the ways they've learned today.

"Today, when you go off to write your Tiny Moments, make sure you are remembering to *go back and try to read your story*. And today, and from this day on, let's all try hard to write stories that could go in your easy-to-read pile."

When you make lists with your children, remember that less is more. Long laundry lists that include everything under the sun aren't helpful. Once you've listed three or four items, your children should be able to continue thinking of more examples on their own without your list becoming too overwhelming to be of much use to anyone.

To support the second item on the list, during an interactive writing lesson later that day, Natalie showed her kids that when they wanted to fix something in their writing, they could simply cross it out. "This is what writers do," she said, and demonstrated.

What a lovely tangible goal! Notice that the link in this minilesson names exactly what you hope all your writers will do today. This is different than usual. Usually the link will remind children of a lesson that may or may not be applicable to that very day. The difference is that requiring children to write so that someone can read their writing doesn't micromanage what they do; they still have their independence. Some will be continuing on a story, others will start with a new story. They'll write on a vast range of topics. But your hope is they'll all take the time to write for readers.

MID-WORKSHOP TEACHING POINT

Share the story of a child who noticed that some aspect of his or her writing was hard to read and fixed it. Ask all the children who "fixed a hard-to-read part of their writing" to raise their hands.

"Hey everyone, could I stop you? Victor just did the most important thing! First, he tried his best to write the beginning sentence of his story. Then he brought that sentence to me and asked if I could read it, and guess what? There was a part of his writing that I couldn't read easily, and you know what Victor did? As soon as I looked confused over a word, he took his pencil, reached right around me, like this, and fixed the word so that it had more of the important sounds in it. Right there. He just fixed it! Then, when he went back to his seat to continue his writing, he kept rereading his writing and he fixed some more! I want all of you to do this while you are writing. Reread, notice, fix it right away and keep going. How many of you already fixed a hard-to-read part of your writing today? Raise your hand. Wow! Let's keep thinking about doing this for our writing tomorrow."

Sometimes after a conference that you believe has relevance for other children, you'll stop the whole class and retell the conference in a way designed to teach others

"Don't you want children to focus on their content, not their correctness?" you may ask. "Don't you want them to postpone concern over correctness until they are editing toward publication?" The truth is that concern over spelling can't be relegated to the editing phase of writing when the writer is five or six years old. Young children will inevitably think about spelling as they try to get their words on the page in the first place. And we do want them to take an extra few seconds to listen for more sounds, to recognize and use familiar chunks, to recall known parts of words. However, it is key to help children balance their attention to meaning and their attention to convention, because we definitely do not want a concern for correctness to interfere with children's dedication to make meaning.

As you confer, you're going to want to get children to reread their writing. You will want to prepare by studying the conferences listed to the right. As you study these conferences, try to notice all the ways in which your presence can help children do the work they need to do. You want *the child* to be the one to look at the pictures and anticipate the content, to hold the paper, to point under words, and to realize that when he or she comes to a hard word it can help to back up, reread, and get a running start. Your presence needs to nudge children to work harder (rather than allowing them to rely on you).

Notice the lean, clean prompts in "Say and Record a Word, Then Reread," and try to be sure that when you teach, your prompts are equally lean. You want to function like training wheels, providing subtle but crucial support in ways that allow children to get up some speed, to carry on with a sense of "I can do this."

Remember that you have a conferring checklist that can help you notice what your children are already doing and decide what you want to teach next. Carry it with you to help you see, celebrate, and plan. If a child seems to be carrying on just fine, remember that you teach when you notice and name what the child is already doing, which you hope the child will continue. If the child is saying words slowly to listen for sounds, then tell that child how smart the child is to be doing this. Then use the conferring checklist to remind you of one thing you could teach.

 These conferences in *The Conferring Handbook* may be especially helpful today:

- ▶ *"Say and Record a Word, Then Reread"*
- ▶ *"If You Erase That Word and Scoot It Over, It Will Be Easier to Read"*

Also, if you have *Conferring with Primary Writers*, you may want to refer to the following conference:

- ▶ *"Reread as You Write, Paying Attention to White Space and Spelling"*

After-the-Workshop Share

Me and my brother was playing Dreamcast. Freddie lost. I win.

Tell the class about a writer who reread and realized she needed to fix up part of her writing.

"Sheena did such a smart thing today during writing. She was trying to decide if a piece of her writing was easy or hard to read and while she was reading it, she came to a part that didn't make sense. Instead of giving up, she said, 'Let me try even harder to read this.' When she tried again she realized that what she had written didn't match what she wanted to say. So she fixed it so that it would say what she wanted it to say." [*Fig. II-1*]

Then Freddie got mad.

I just stood there.

Fig. II-1   Sheena

Ask the children to try to read their writing and decide if it goes in the easy- or hard-to-read pile.

"All of us, like Sheena, need to be honest about whether our writing is readable. Being honest will help us make our writing better. Right now, would each one of you look at the writing you did today and decide, 'Should today's writing go in the easy-to-read pile or the hard-to-read pile?' If it would go in the hard-to-read pile, see if there is *one little* part of your writing that you think you could fix up the way Sheena did and put a star near that part. *Then* you can start on it first thing tomorrow, and make it easier to read!"

The cohesive quality of these minilessons is impressive. In Session I, Natalie talks about encountering hard-to-read writing; in Session II children divide their work into these categories. Now after the workshop on Session II, Natalie returns to the concept of there being two piles, easy and hard-to-read, and asks children to assess their newest work and to file it in the right category. Some children will find their writing is still hard to read—so it was brilliant of Natalie to ask these youngsters to find one part that they could make a little bit easier to read and to use that as a starting point for the next day!

IF CHILDREN NEED MORE TIME

You may decide to break this session into two halves. One minilesson could emphasize that we study the picture and recall what we know about a topic before trying to read the print. The other minilesson could be about the strategic work we do with print when we *really* want to read something. This latter minilesson could teach children to reread in order to recall what they've written, to notice the first letter of a puzzling word, and to think "What could it say?" Rather than highlighting specific reading strategies children could use when they encounter difficulty, the minilesson could spotlight the importance of readers being resourceful and active, persevering in the face of difficulty rather than just giving up. Perhaps you could role-play a child who at first gave up, saying, "I can't read that!" and who then said, "Wait. Let me try harder," and this time, pulled in close, used a lot of strategies, and met with success. Perhaps you could liken good reading to the story *The Little Engine That Could*. The engine said "I think I can, I think I can, I think I can," and with determination, managed to chug over the mountain.

When you look over your children's work, pay very close attention, training your eye to see the small steps that each writer has made. Your attentiveness to these small steps will support progress more than anything else you can do. Be sure you gush to each child over any sign of progress that you see, and help the child regard this as an indication of great promise. If you have trouble seeing progress, be sure to remember that often a child's work will be partly wrong but also partly right. Even when the child's spellings are problematic, there can be evidence of progress.

Discipline yourself to pay attention to the child's artwork. The artwork often holds the key to the child's meaning, and your close scrutiny and easy delight in the pictures will balance the goal-orientation of this unit and help you and your children remember that letters and sounds are just a piece of the total package of communicating the many interesting, powerful, and wonderful stories the children have inside them.

For example, look closely at Consuela's story in Figure II-2. Her sentences reflect the struggles English Language Learners often have with verbs and transitional clauses. Like other English Language Learners, she sometimes holds tight to present tense verbs (My Mom said to go to bed so I go to bed), and she writes with simple, sparse sentences strung together with conjunctions. Yet her drawings show that she's eager to write in ways that bring the pulse and detail and color of her life onto the page! Notice the stars surrounding her mother, the details of her mother's outfit and of the plate in her mother's hand. Then, on page two, notice how the drawing brings out the internal story that does not yet fit into Consuela's prose.

Because Consuela's pictures contain more story than do her words do, it is easy for me to teach how to add details to her writing. The detail in the pictures gives me an idea to teach Consuela to use her pictures to help her with hard-to-read words.

Fig. II-2   Consuela

I went to my mom and my mom said, "You have to eat food."
My mom said to go to bed. So I go to bed and I said, "I do not want to go to bed."
So I went to my room anyway.

STRETCHING AND WRITING WORDS

GETTING READY

- A class Tiny Moment story told in pictures on a chart paper booklet
- One set of wipe-off boards, markers, and an eraser (a sock) distributed to each child or, if necessary, to each pair of children
- See CD-ROM for resources

IN YOUR CONFERENCES, *you will have worked hard to help children listen for and record sounds. Now you'll bring this focus into your minilesson.*

Your assessments of your children should greatly influence any minilessons you teach that focus on letters and sounds. In some classrooms, and especially in kindergarten rooms, it would be challenging enough to encourage children to listen not only beginning but also ending sounds in words they want to write. In other classrooms, children will be ready to study the spelling of the word battle *or* little *and notice the /el/ sound is actually spelled* le, *collecting other words which follow that spelling pattern—teaching not only a spelling pattern but also the lesson that spellers use known words to help with new words. You'll need to revise this minilesson so that it is right for your children.*

At this time in the year, Natalie's children find it challenging to hear and record the major sounds in a word. In this minilesson, therefore, Natalie encourages her children to hear and record more sounds in the words they write.

The Minilesson

Connection

Remind the children that they have been trying to write for readers. Tell them that today you will show them one thing to help them write easier-to-read words.

"Hey everyone, for the past couple of days, we have been trying to write easy-to-read Tiny Moment stories. While you have been writing, I know you are asking, 'Will Ms. Louis be able to read this?' 'Can Lucy read this?' and, 'Can *I* read this?' Sometimes your words are hard to read because you only write down one letter or two for a word. Today I'm going to show you how writers stretch out some of our words and hear a lot of sounds in them. You'll see that we say the word, write a sound, reread what we've written, and say the word again. There's a lot of going backwards, *then* going forward, then going backwards, then going forward. I'll show you what I mean."

Whenever you can, use gestures to accompany your words. So when you describe going backwards (and mean going back to reread), act out how you back up to the start of the word to reread it—this helps kids who listen better when there are visuals accompanying the oral language, and it especially helps your English language learners.

Teaching

Read the picture story you have written, saying aloud the short sentences you plan to write publicly.

"I have drawn a story across three pages about a tiny moment that happened in our class. Watch and listen as I turn the pages and tell the story, like you do before you write." Touching page one, Natalie said, "'We had a show for our families.'" She turned the page. "'We stood on stage and waited to start. We each found someone to wave to.'" She turned the page. "'We waved, smiled together on the stage, and we sang too.' That's my tiny moment, drawn across three pages."

Whenever possible, it is great for you to write your stories about events the class experienced together rather than about your own private affairs. Although Natalie will focus on hearing and recording sounds, she is also teaching narrative craft. This demonstration reminds children to draw first, to touch pages and say their stories, and to write about tiny, focused, true events. Natalie need not talk about these things; she is teaching them whether or not she does so explicitly.

Write publicly in a way that demonstrates what you want children to notice and tackle for themselves. In this case, emphasize tackling hard words by rereading frequently.

"First I'm going to label my picture. We stood on the stage, so I want to write *stage*. Watch how I write *stage*: I say the word. *Stage*. I say it again and listen for the start of the word. *Stage*. I hear /st/. So I think, what can I write that will spell /st/ like in *stage* . . . or *stop*? I remember stop: s-t-o-p! So I write *st*. Now watch, I read what I've written." Natalie put her finger under the *st* and read that.

"Before I go on, would you say the word *stage* and see if you can hear the sounds at the start of the word like I did and write the letters down on your wipe boards?" The children all took their dry erase boards and soon they'd written *st*. "Put your fingers under what you've written. That's what writers do. Read what you've written . . . and then *say the rest of the word* and listen for what sound comes next."

Soon most children had said *age* and isolated and recorded the /a/ sound. "Again, writers, let's read what we've written, *sta*, and say what comes next."

"I heard st*age—/age/*." Natalie wrote the remaining letters without commentary because they were probably too difficult for many of her children. "Writers, did you see how I kept saying the word, writing down what I heard, then rereading it and saying more of the word?"

Active Engagement

Ask children to try the writing work you have just done in front of them. In this case, tell them to try writing a certain word by rereading frequently.

"Let's try labeling the audience by writing the word *people* over them, okay? First you need to say *people* slowly and listen to the sounds you hear at the start of the word. Write those down, then reread with your finger and see how many more sounds you can hear and record. Do this now."

It may not be spellbinding to read this transcript but don't let yourself skim past this. The moves that Natalie makes in this minilesson are as important for you to learn as anything else in this series of books. If you can learn how to teach children to listen for, record, and read the sounds they hear in a word, you are well on your way to teaching children to write and to read.

One of the best indicators that a child is ready to take off as a reader is that the child writes in such a way that a literate adult can reread the child's writing—and the child can reread his or her writing with one-to-one matching. You don't want to fold your hands and wait for this to happen "developmentally." You need to teach toward this. This transcript and others like it will equip you to do so.

It isn't an accident that you've set your children up with a relatively easy word to spell. (It's not easy if you aim for correctness, but if you aim for a good approximation it's not hard.)

Link

Remind writers to try what they've learned today and every day—saying words slowly and rereading until they can read the whole word from the page.

"Writers, today and every day, when you work on writing your own stories, try to do like we've been doing when you come to hard words. Say them slowly, hear the first sounds, and write those down; then *reread with your finger under the letter and hear more sounds*. I'll admire the work you do. And, anyone who feels that they need a little more practice with me to work on writing more letters in a word, those people should stay on the rug and we will practice another word together before you go off to write."

Notice that a minilesson such as this doesn't set children up for the major work they'll be doing on this day. The minilesson hasn't addressed the subject of what children will write or the genre they'll choose. The teacher assumes that children have ongoing work to do in the writing workshop and assumes also that they can proceed with initiative and independence in their ongoing work. If this causes a problem, the best solution is to teach children to rise to this challenge rather than allowing them to rely on you to set up the specific course of their work each day. For example, you could ask children before the start of the minilesson to tell their partner what they plan to do as writers today, and use this as a time to remind them that they should have plans. Alternatively, each day at the end of writing workshop, you could ask writers to put tomorrow's work in the right-hand side of their folders and to make themselves a reminder note of what they plan to do the next day so they'll be ready to start without needing directions from you.

TIME TO CONFER

In your conferences, you'll probably encourage your children to hear and record the major sounds in words that are unfamiliar to them. As you do so, keep in mind the hints for helping children say words slowly, listening to and recording the sounds they hear. You'll find this list of hints more fully described on the CD-ROM, *Resources for Primary Writing*.

Hints for helping children say words slowly and listen to the sounds:

▶ You want *the child* to be the one to say the word slowly. *Don't take over this job for the child!*

▶ It's a sign of great progress if a child begins to hear more sounds in a word even if the child doesn't yet know the letters that match those sounds.

▶ Expect children to hear and record consonants before vowels.

▶ You want children to stretch out words, saying them slowly, but to do this without turning every word into a line of staccato sounds. If children make words staccato, they sometimes hear extra consonants, as does the child who stretches out *dog* like this: *dah-ow-gah*.

▶ When you want to help children hear and record vowels, teach "the vowel cluster" (or "the rime").

These conferences in *The Conferring Handbook* may be especially helpful today:

▶ *"Say and Record a Word, Then Reread"*

▶ *"If You Erase That Word and Scoot It Over, It Will Be Easier to Read"*

▶ *"Famous Writers Use Periods to Tell Readers Where to Stop"*

Also, if you have *Conferring with Primary Writers*, you may want to refer to the conferences in part three.

Convene the children. Ask them to select one hard word they wrote, to reread it, and to have a friend reread it.

"Would you find a word you wrote today that was a hard word, and see if you can reread it now? Put your finger underneath the word and read all the letters like this." I did it with *recess*. "You may find you can add another letter, recording another sound! Show the word to a friend and see if your friend can read it. If your friend has trouble, tell your friend to do like smart readers do and study the picture first, then try again to read it."

▶ The reason for writing *stage* and *people* was that these words belonged in a story the class was helping you create. Another day you could ask children to help a fellow classmate. "Willy has drawn this story about getting stuck in the elevator and now he wants to label his picture but he needs help on some of his words. Let's help him out."

▶ You could point out that sometimes you see kids acting like adventuresome spellers, going for a harder-to-spell word, with precisely the right meaning instead of just writing the word they know already that isn't quite right. "Let's practice being brave spellers!" you could say. The class could then generate a list of words, like *hippopotamus*, and learn to break down first by clapping the syllables, then by tackling one bit at a time.

▶ You could give tips on stretching out words. You might say, "I've been listening to all of you stretching words out so you can spell them and some of you talk like robots. You want to write *rattlesnake* so you say it like this 'ra-ta-le-sna-ak-ka.' I can tell you are trying to do the right thing but actually, great spellers say the words slowly but not in robot-talk. Here is the trick. We can say the whole word—*rattlesnake*—slowly and listen for the first sounds or for the next sound. Let's try it. Say *rattlesnake* slowly and then tell your friend the first sound in the word." They would. "Now say *rattlesnake* slowly and tell your friend the next sound." And so on.

▶ You might tell kids to look at the letters they've written so far so that actually, they are reading half the word, and then saying the other half of it. If a child who wants to record *rattlesnake* tracks the word along the letters he's already written, *ratlsn*, then he knows what to write next.

WRITING WITH SIGHT WORDS

GETTING READY

▸ Last session's chart paper story, complete with pictures and labels

● See CD-ROM for resources

IN THE LAST SESSION, YOUR CHILDREN HELPED *you begin writing the words to accompany a Tiny Moment story. You labeled the drawing and helped children stretch words out, listening for the sounds. In this session, you and the class will continue to work on the same story. This time you'll write a sentence to accompany your drawing and in doing so, you'll remind children that writers rely on sight words (not just stretching words and recording the sounds) to write.*

This minilesson is one you'll repeat several times and you'll use versions of it as small group strategy lessons. Whenever you teach a version of this minilesson, you'll want to decide which strategy to highlight, based on what you see your children reading. You may, for example, not listen for and record sounds as Natalie does here, but instead hear and record parts of words that are familiar to you. "Oh! I know that chunk. It's the same as in (cite the word)." You may also come to words that are in the classroom and show children how you copy those words.

In this minilesson, you remind writers that while they stretch out some words, recording the sounds, there are other words they know instantly.

THE MINILESSON

Connection

Remind children of yesterday's work and recruit them to continue writing the story. Tell them that writers use strategies other than stretching out words.

"Yesterday all of you helped me label my story. We wrote *stage* and *people*," Natalie said, pointing to the words. "We wrote a bit of the word, then reread what we'd written, then heard more sounds. Today, let's work on the same story."

"You'll see that I stretch *some* words out (like we did yesterday), but writers use other strategies, too. Today, I will teach you how writers write faster by switching back and forth from writing words slowly by stretching them out and writing words faster because they already know how to spell them."

Teaching

Model for children how you resume writing by studying yesterday's work and recalling what you planned to say. Touch the pages and say what you plan to write.

"Sometimes when it is time to add on to yesterday's work, I find I've forgotten what I already wrote! Does that ever happen to you?" Natalie asked. Then she said, "So I usually begin by remembering what I'm going to be writing, don't you? Let's go back and look at what we have so far." She looked at her drawing on page one and page two. "Oh, yeah, remember? It'll go . . . " And she touched page one. "'We had a show for our families.'" She turned the page. "'We stood on the stage and waited to start. We each found someone to wave to.'" She turned the page. "'We waved, smiled together on the stage, and we sang too!'"

Ask the children to watch how you write the words. Show them that you write the words you know with automaticity, and talk about this.

Pointing to the first page of her chart-paper booklet, Natalie said, "Now, I need to write the words for my story. You heard me say the words, but it is much harder work to get those words down on the page! Watch how I write words." Pointing to the first page, Natalie said, "I need to write, 'We had a show for our families.'"

Today, Natalie will be teaching children that they should have a repertoire of words they know with automaticity. These tend to be high-frequency words. She searches for child-appropriate ways to explain the usefulness of having this repertoire of words you "just know."

Minilessons generally make one teaching point, and the teacher names that point by the end of the Connection. The point of this minilesson is that writers vary their strategies for spelling a word. Instead of making a beeline for this point, Natalie makes a detour—she does this because when she and I were planning this minilesson, we found ourselves needing to reorient ourselves to the work we'd done the day before. We are in the habit of paying attention to any struggle we have, because children will tend to run into the same struggles when they work on their own. In this detour Natalie names the struggle ("Sometimes when it is time to add on to yesterday's work, I find I've forgotten what I was working on! Does that ever happen to you?") We want kids to know that when they struggle in this way, it's time to reach for a solution ("Let me show you what I do when I am about to add onto yesterday's writing. I always begin by remembering what I was writing about. . . .").

She said that line again, "We had a show for our families."

"Watch how I write the words," Natalie said, and she repeated her sentence and then wrote the first three words quickly, muttering as she did so, "I *know* these words." Then, in a brief aside, she commented to the children, "Did you see that? I wrote those words in a snap," she snapped her fingers, "because I just know them. What if *you* had to write *mom*, would you have to stretch it out and sound it out? No! You could write it in a snap."

Returning to her line of print, Natalie said, "Now, remember that we often reread what we have written. Help me. '*We had a. . . .*'"

Demonstrate writing some of your words slowly, staying close to the previous session's model.

"The next word I need to write is *show*. *Show*. Watch what I do right here. I say the word again. *Show*. What is the first sound I hear? /sh/."

"Then I think, 'What letter makes the /sh/ sound? (The children say c-h.) "We answer a c-h. So I write a c-h."

"Now, let me read what I have written so far." Natalie put her finger under the words and she read them. "'We had a /sh/, /sh/- (ow)."

Active Engagement

Recruit the children to help you with the next sounds, to reread with you, to say the next sound, and to record what they hear, then to reread again.

"Will you help me with the next sounds?" Natalie asked. "First we need to again say the word *show*. We've already written the /sh/ sound so listen and let's think, 'What sound do we hear next?' Say *show* to yourself quietly while we look at the letters we've written." The children do this, isolating the /ow/ sound. "What letters make that sound? Suggestions?"

Natalie's point will be to teach children that there are some words she "just knows" and, therefore, can write quickly. She could have just said this to her children and showed them the same is true for them. But she wants to demonstrate how this fits into the process of composing a story, so she resumes writing, attending to meaning, and expeditiously gets to the point she wants to make.

Natalie could say, "I hear an s-h," (referring to the letters by name), but she had asked, "What sound do I hear?" so the answer is /sh/. It's wise to keep our terms straight, remembering that children rely on us to teach them what we mean by "a letter."

Of course, show is spelled with an sh not a ch. Each of you will need to decide whether you feel comfortable demonstrating spellings that aren't perfect. Our rule of thumb is that if the point of the demonstration is not spelling but something else, such as adding details, we spell correctly and don't make a big deal out of this. If our lesson is on the strategies writers use to spell (as this one is), we work in the far range of what the class can do. When we are demonstrating how to go about spelling words, we do what we hope our children will do (but we don't operate at a level that is light years beyond what they can do.) Remember that at the start of this year, half of Natalie's children didn't know even eight letters by name or sound. Natalie knows that putting ch for sh is a pretty smart mistake and doesn't want to get into a long explanation of the difference in sound between the ch and the sh. This is a teacher's judgment call. Natalie could have said, "It does sound kind of like a ch, doesn't it, but actually it is an sh."

Willy said, "I hear a /o/ like snow." Willy was referring to the snow on their letter flashcards.

"Good. What letter makes that sound?"

"An O."

Show children how you reread often in the midst of writing.

"Now let's reread what we have so far for this word and decide if we have enough letters to say /sho/- /w/. Is this word finished? Do you hear any more sounds?"

"Okay. Now is the word done? Let's put our finger under it and reread. /show/. How does that look and sound? Do you hear any more sounds that need a letter in that word?"

"No."

Gradually remove your scaffolding support so that children work with more independence.

"Alright, now it's time for the next word. Reread all the words we have so far and tell your partner what's next."

The children did this and told Natalie that *for* is next. "Good. The word *for* is next. We know *for* and it's on our word wall. Point to it, class, so let's just write it in a snap. Write it on your hand while I write it here." They did. "What's next—tell your partner. Good—I see you rereading!" The children called out *the*. "We know *the*, spell it on your hand." They did, writing with a finger. "We'll finish tomorrow, but I love the way you just write some words like *for* and *the* in a snap and other words you stretch out! Writers do that. When we write words in a snap, we hear the word we need to write, and then we check to see if a picture of the word pops up in our head, or we listen to see if we hear the list of letters like a chart in our minds. Then we write what we see from the picture, or we record the letters we hear in our memory."

This process will feel very slow, but it becomes more fluid as children move from hearing and recording sounds one letter at a time to hearing and recording chunks.

The children in this instance didn't hear the /w/ sound in show. This is typical for early spellers. Our goal right now was to teach these children to listen for the sounds they hear and record those. A teacher could tuck in a w saying, "Actually there is a w there," as if it's not big deal. Don't insist that the whole class hear the w because this gives the message that spelling requires the teacher's step-by-step assistance. We don't want to convey that message.

It is more efficient and effective to spell by analogies than to listen for single sounds—and you'll watch Natalie teach this over the course of this unit.

Here Natalie refers to the word wall. Earlier, when Natalie's children said they heard an /o/ as in snow, they were referring to their alphabet chart and accompanying flash cards. Writing workshop gives children a chance to use what they learn in other times of the day, but it can't be the only place children learn letter-sound correspondence.

Natalie wisely ends her demonstration by emphasizing writing some words "in a snap" because this was the point she wanted to make today.

Link

Remind children to remember today and always, that there are some words they can write in a snap. For other words, they can use the same exact steps that they did together on the rug.

"Today everyone, when you are writing your own stories, you'll write some words in a snap and some words you'll stretch out like we did with *show*. You will be switching back and forth between those two different ways to write the words in your story. When a word pops into your head like a picture or like a chant, then you should write that word in a snap without sounding it out. The chant and the picture in your mind mean that you probably already know how to spell this word. If you know a word is on our word wall, you should be able to write it in a snap. If you can't, use the word wall to fix your memory of that word, and then try to write it correctly. Make sure you check your spelling by looking at the word wall after you have tried writing that word on your own. Who is ready to write their words like we did today? Shavon is ready. His table can go, too. Lilly is ready. Her table can go. Sheena and her table. Everyone else."

MID-WORKSHOP TEACHING POINT

Recruit the class to help one child with a tricky word.

"Just now I saw Maria trying to write *spaghetti*. Let's all see if we can help her. Try writing *spaghetti* on the back of your story. Help each other."

The children did this. "I love noticing the strategies you used to write your tricky word. Thumbs up if you said the word over to yourself, like Timor did when he said, 'fountain.' Next, Timor listened for the first sound and wrote that. Thumbs up if you did the same thing. Great! Then Timor *reread* what he'd written, with his finger under the word, like this, '/f/(ountain).' Thumbs up if you did that. Did you say the word again? You all did some great work. Use these strategies always when you come to tricky words."

If a word is on the word wall and a child has forgotten how to spell it, we encourage the child to look at the word, notice the letters, fix them in her mind, say them aloud, check that she has them, write them, and check what she's written against the posted word. That is, we encourage the child to learn rather than to copy the word from the word wall.

As children become more proficient in spelling, they will hear and record chunks rather than phonemes. Eventually, Timor will hear "/foun/," not "/f/." Natalie's class is a homogeneous one, full of children who have been classified as at-risk readers, and she is quite sure that for most of them right now, it is challenging enough to teach them to tackle long words and to listen for dominant sounds. If you believe this work is only pertinent for a small group, this mid-workshop teaching point could be turned into a small group strategy lesson.

Today, your goal is to help as many kids as possible try to write words using the steps that you taught during the minilesson.

Remember that you don't want to do most of the work for the child, nor do you want to talk on and on about what the child is expected to do. Think of yourself as a coach. Move alongside the writer as he or she works. Interject lean, concise prompts that remind the writer what to do. The writer wants to write dinner and has written a *d.* Now the writer sits, paralyzed, unsure of what comes next. Just say, "Reread with your finger." Don't do this rereading work for or with the child. If the child has trouble, you can decide to demonstrate. "Watch how I reread with my finger." Then pass the baton over to the child. Say, "Now you do it," and don't say more unless the child gets stymied. Even then, try to just say one lean, concise prompt and then back away.

It is key to allow approximation. If you realize that the child who is writing *dinner* doesn't know the er chunk and you believe the child should know this chunk, you still need not make a fuss about this right here and now. If you are meanwhile trying to help this child make progress in his ability to record what he hears in a self-sufficient manner, you'd be wise to tuck away your plan to teach the *er* chunk, planning to teach it at another time. If your message is, "You can do this, just use these few strategies," then be sure you don't inadvertently convey, "If you do this on your own, you'll mess up, so be sure I'm near to show you exactly the right way."

These conferences in *The Conferring Handbook* may be especially helpful today:

▶ *"Say and Record a Word, Then Reread"*
▶ *"If You Erase That Word and Scoot It Over, It Will Be Easier to Read"*
▶ *"Famous Writers Use Periods to Tell Readers Where to Stop"*

Also, if you have *Conferring with Primary Writers*, you may want to refer to the conferences in part three.

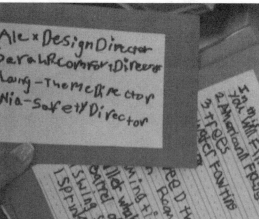

After-the-Workshop Share

Have the kids try to write a word from one of their classmates' writing using the same process you demonstrated in the minilesson. This time follow the chart, below:

"Writers, I watched so many of you using our word-writing strategies," Natalie gestured toward a chart she had written the night before, "to write your words today. Let's all try using these strategies one more time with one of Lilly's words. Lilly needed help with *kitten*. Will you work with your friend to try to spell *kitten* on the back of one of your stories? Let's follow the steps."

WORD WRITING STEPS

1. Say the word two times
2. Hear the first sound. Spell that sound
3. Read it. Say the next part of the word. Write that
4. Hear the next sound. Spell that sound
5. Repeat steps three and four until you can't hear any more sounds
6. Reread it

Natalie read step one. "Okay, do that," she said, and gave them a minute to say *kitten* twice to their partner. Natalie then continued reading, again leaving a space for them to do the next step, and this continued until they'd written *kitten*.

"Good work, writers. Now try using these strategies again, just you and your friend, with Marcela's word, *skateboard*. From now on use these strategies when you come to words you don't know."

Notice the way Natalie brings a chart into her teaching. In this instance, she taught her writers to use a series of strategies, then made the strategies into a chart at home. She tucks the chart into this share session, showing children that they can use the chart to remind them of the process. The important thing is that Natalie doesn't confuse charting with teaching. Often I see minilessons in which making a chart is the main event, with the teaching writing each bit of the chart out as children watch. The making of a chart can't be the heart of a minilesson. Charts are a way to record and recall what one has learned—but making a chart isn't usually a powerful way to teach.

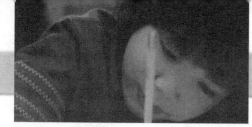

- Do the same minilesson again, using a wider variety of strategies to determine the letters you plan to write. You may listen for chunks. You may use analogies to other known words. You can also show what to do if you don't know how to record a sound. "Hmm. I don't know that sound. I'll leave a question mark for now and later I'll ask someone."

- Pull children together into small-group strategy lessons, and ask them to help one child with his or her story. They can all use paper or a wipe board and work simultaneously, step-by-step, through the words the child wants to write.

- Vary the minilesson by having children all record the letters either on their own paper or on white boards.

- Turn the share session into a minilesson. Perhaps, instead of providing a chart of the strategies writers use to spell words, solicit the class to help make such a chart. ("Let's make a chart on what writers do when they are stuck on a spelling.") Then teach the class to use the chart.

- Use a piece of text from an interactive writing you did earlier in the day and talk about how some words we write fast like a rabbit—have your kids hold up two fingers like rabbit ears—and some words we write slowly like a turtle—have your kids hold up a fist like a turtle in his shell. Go through the already written text together recalling whether a word was written quickly or slowly. Have children use their rabbit and turtle hand motions to identify quickly and slowly. Later, you can check in on your writers' process of recording words just by asking writers to hold up finger-ears or a fist-shell.

SPACING WORDS

GETTING READY

- Sentence from last session and start of next sentence.
- Set of wipe-off boards, markers, and an eraser (a sock) for every child.
- Words from one page of a familiar Big Book copied with no spaces between words (*Mrs. Wishy-Washy*)
- Big Book itself (*Mrs. Wishy-Washy*)
- See CD-ROM for resources

IN THIS SESSION, YOU WILL HELP CHILDREN *put spaces between words. It isn't hard to understand that spaces between words are helpful. However, it can be hard for a child to figure out what is and what isn't a whole word— the stream of sounds that constitutes spoken language doesn't come with spaces between words. How can a child know when one word ends and the next word begins? Don't be surprised to find that it can be more difficult for children to leave spaces between words than it is for them to record the sounds they hear within words.*

No single lesson will teach children how to do this. Think of today's work as consciousness-raising, and continue to support this concept in small group and one-to-one forums during writing, reading, and other subject areas. Expect that some of your children, and especially many of your kindergarten children, will probably be working toward control of one-to-one matching for at least another month.

In this lesson, you'll teach children that it's important to leave a finger-sized blank space when they hear no more sounds in a word.

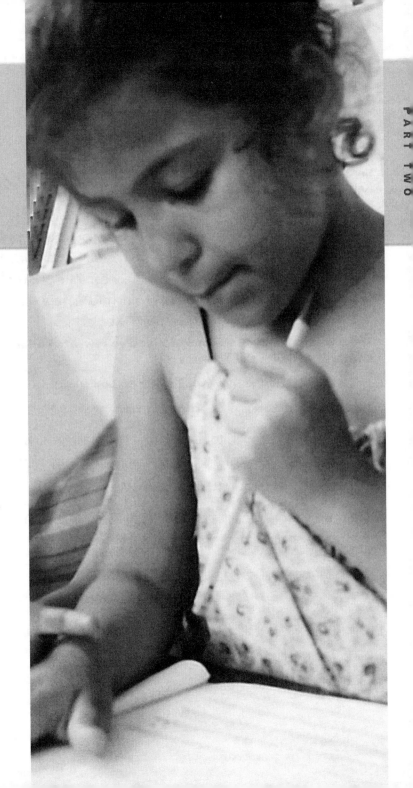

THE MINILESSON

Connection

Remind children that they've been writing the sounds they hear. Tell them that this can help them to put spaces between words.

"Okay everyone, yesterday, while you were writing your Tiny Moment stories, and you came to a word that you couldn't spell in a snap, you stretched that word out. You wrote all of the sounds that you heard. Keep doing that today and every day. When you concentrate on writing all of the sounds in a word, this can help you know when to leave a space. Today, we are going to learn to put spaces between our words."

Show children a Big Book in which you've rewritten a familiar line without spaces. Contrast this with the actual text.

"Let me show you how important spaces are for readers. What does this say?"

IntothetubyougosaidMrsWishyWashy

"It's tough to read, isn't it?" Natalie peeled off her rendition of the text, leaving the original words showing. "Now try to read this one:

'Into the tub you go,' said Mrs. Wishy-Washy.

That's much easier to read, isn't it? So today I'll show you how to write with spaces."

Notice the nice, clear message about what the children will learn today. You should come to expect this in the last line or two of the connection. In this Connection, Natalie tells and shows children what she will teach. She doesn't fool herself into thinking that the second portion of this connection is sufficient to be her teaching component.

Throughout these minilessons, you'll see that when we want to highlight one feature of a written text, we do so by juxtaposing that text with another version which the author could have written. Here, Cowley could have cramped her words together, leaving no white space between words, but instead, she left white space. During the Small Moments unit, Abby pointed out that she could write about the fire drill without providing any details, but with children's help, she instead wrote the story in all its detail. In these and many other instances, the juxtaposition of two versions of a text helps draw attention to the one feature we're trying to highlight.

Teaching

Tell children that when they are writing and they have come to where there are no more sounds to listen for, they leave a space.

When you are writing words carefully, you keep asking yourself the question, "What sound do I hear next?" Then you write the letter that makes that sound. When you ask yourself, "What sound do I hear next?" and your answer is, "No more sounds," then you know that you are at the end of the word and it is time to leave a space before you say a new word. It's like spaces are the rest that you give yourself and your pencil and your paper before you tackle the next word."

Active Engagement

Ask children to finish last session's text on white boards, leaving spaces. Help them record a phrase, adding spaces after each word.

"Each of you has your own wipe-off board. Remember that last time we wrote about the show? We wrote, 'We had a show for our families. We stood on stage. . . .' You are going to use your white board to try to write the rest of our sentence with spaces in the right places. We'll help each other. Remember, a space between words is like a resting place. It should be just big enough for your finger to fit into (but you don't need to put your finger down to measure it, just make it about that big)."

"Let's read what we have so far. We wrote, 'We stood on the stage.' Today we need to write, 'and waited to start.' Turn your boards the long way like this and write *and* on the beginning of your boards. Good. Read what you've written. Did you come to the end of *and*? Do you hear any more sounds? If you don't hear more sounds, you are done with the word and your paper needs a rest, a space. Give your board a rest now, a space."

"What's next, *we*? Write that. When you come to where there are no more sounds in *we*, let your paper rest, leave a space. Now, I want you to try to write the rest of the sentence on your boards: 'waited to start.'"

Children set to work. Some referred to the chart of word-writing steps from yesterday's share. As a result, they were writing words that were more

Many of us would have been content to show the line from Mrs. Wishy-Washy written without and then with spaces. But Natalie understands that assigning children to do something isn't teaching them to do it. To teach, she finds words the children will understand to describe a process that often goes untaught.

Notice that Natalie has one main point to her minilesson but this doesn't stop her from tucking a few subordinate pointers into the lesson. She need not have an entirely separate minilesson detailing the size of space writers leave between words.

Don't hesitate to reuse terms over and over. Natalie is wise to repeat the idea that the white space gives the paper a rest.

Watch that Natalie at first provided a lot of scaffolding for her students to get them started. Now she is withdrawing some of that support—lifting up the training wheels—and helping her children carry on with a bit more independence. This sequence is a beautiful progression and one we, as teachers, need to rely on constantly.

readable than we'd usually seen. Other kids did not seem to be doing any rereading at all. Some children were writing letters that had no apparent connection to the word they were trying to write.

Solicit children's help in writing the rest of the text on your chart paper, recording sounds and spaces.

"Everyone, let me stop you. Cap your pens. Look at this story up here. Help me write the next sentence with all the letters and with the spaces. Tell me what you have written and I will write it here."

Joe began, "I know *and* like that," he snapped his fingers, "so, I wrote it a-n-d, then made a space."

"Then I wrote *we*, w-e," Daniel added.

Natalie wrote w-e, "Do you hear any more sounds in *we*?" she asked and when the children chorused that they didn't, Natalie said, "So we'll leave a space." Then the class followed the lead of her pointer and reread in unison, starting at the beginning of the story. "We had a concert for our families. We stood on the stage and we. . . ." Natalie led the class through the writing of the next words, with kids chiming in along the way. At each word end, she asked "Do you hear any other sounds in the word *waited*?" When the children said no, she reminded them to leave a space as a rest.

Tell children you'll finish the writing later (strategically recruit a small group of children who could use extra guided practice to stay and help).

"Okay. Nicole suggests there's no more sounds in *waited*, so we should give the paper a rest with a space. I will finish writing this as you do your writing. Juliser and Sebastian, will you stay and help me?"

Link

Remind children to leave spaces between their words. Refer back to the cramped and well-spaced text from the beginning of the lesson.

"Today and every day when you write, put spaces between your words. Don't write like this," she showed 'IntothetubyougosaidMrsWishyWashy,' "but write like this: 'Into the tub you go,' said Mrs. Wishy-Washy.'"

Remember that it's easier to get children's mental attention if you have them look at you. The comment, "Look at this story up here," is a way of asking for their attention.

Of course, Natalie knew the answer was no, after the w-e children didn't hear more sounds in we, but the whole point of this is that when a writer hears no more sounds, that's the place for a bit of white space. So she makes a point of asking children if they hear more sounds, and when the answer is "no," she leaves a space. Natalie's point is to highlight white space. Her goal isn't, at this moment, to teach the exactly correct spelling for any one word, so she lets her children's approximations go for now and makes a mental note to teach certain things another time.

You'll notice that often the end of a minilesson wraps back to the start, which makes sense because in both places the teacher explicitly names the teaching point.

"When you are listening to the sounds in words, and finish writing them, then you know that it is time to leave a space. Who is ready to try this in their own writing? Off you go blue table. Orange table. Red table. Everyone else."

MID-WORKSHOP TEACHING POINT

Ask children to check to make sure they have left spaces between words. Tell them to use slashes if they haven't.

"Writers, may I stop you all? Would you get your fingers out and use them to reread what you've written so far? Be sure you left spaces between words. If you jammed words together you can fix this quickly for now with slashes like I did here: I/LOV/YOU. Touch each word with your finger, adding slashes if you need to. If you used slashes to mark your spaces, make sure you try to just leave the spaces when you write your next sentence."

It is wise to show children that the reason to write with spaces is that this helps people read their writing. Natalie makes this point by shifting from writing to reading.

TIME TO CONFER

As you confer, watch writers in the process of writing. Because primary children can't always accurately explain their process, you need to observe what they are doing. Three children could all write strings of letters that appear, at a glance, to be similar, but each child could, in fact, be working in dramatically different ways. Does the child say one word at a time, suggesting the child knows what a word is and simply forgets the spaces? Does another child neglect spaces out of an eagerness to move on quickly, to get a lot done? When this child does reread (perhaps with your nudging), does she show any recognition that spacing is a problem? If you nudge the child to do so, can she find, after the fact, where the spaces should have been? If so, you may want the child to insert slashes although you never want a child to write with this from the start. See the conference listed to the right.

You'll find that a few children persist in having problems leaving white spaces between their words. For a few weeks, get these children to say the sentence they want to write (I went to the park) and then, as they say each word, to make a line for that word on their page (____ ____ ____ ____ ____). You'll see, in this piece for example, that Christopher wrote the blanks for his text and then filled in the spellings of words as best he could. [*Fig. V-1*]

Fig. V-1 Christopher

This conference in *The Conferring Handbook* may be especially helpful today:

▶ *"If You Erase That Word and Scoot It Over, It Will Be Easier to Read"*

Also, if you have *Conferring with Primary Writers*, you may want to refer to the following conference:

▶ "Reread as You Write, Paying Attention to White Space and Spelling"

AFTER-THE-WORKSHOP SHARE

Show the writing of a child who fixed a spacing problem. Ask children what they notice.

"Everyone, I need to show you the work that Shawn did today during writing workshop." Natalie had copied his first effort up onto the chart paper on her easel. In this draft, his words were still squished together. Under this draft, Natalie put his second, rewritten version. "What do you notice about the changes he made in his first sentence?" It looked like this:

Iwnto the shostr witmid ad.
I wn to the shostr wit mi dad.
(I went to the shoe store with my dad.)

Marcela said, "He moved the *d* in *dad* so that it was next to the other letters because that is how you write the word *dad*, d-a-d."

Shawn said, "He put in the word to because his sentence didn't make sense without it."

Alain blurted out, "Hey, what's that really long word *shostr* [shoe store]? What's that mean? Oh. I see. It shouldn't be a long word. It should say shoe store. Oh. I get it now."

Natalie didn't want to get lost in the details again so she simply said, "I love seeing all of you think about this. It'll make a huge difference for you. Look how he fixed his spaces so we can tell where the words are!"

Tell children to make their own spacing just right.

"Right now, will each of you get out your writing from today and see if you—like Shawn—can make the spacing as good as it can be?"

It is great to celebrate work that still has lots of problems. The message is clear. We're ready to celebrate hard work and progress and don't expect perfection.

Don't feel that you need to talk much. You showed children the evidence that one child did a lot of work in order to make his text more readable and asked them to take a moment to name what that child did. It doesn't matter if their list is comprehensive. You are teaching writers the gesture of self-assessment and now want them to transfer this to their own text.

Work individually and in small groups with the children who need more time. Your goal at first will be for them to clap or count the number of words in a sentence. You may need to demonstrate, to do this for them. You will probably need to accept approximations. It's far less important that children are correct in hearing *every* separation between words and more important that they grasp the general notion that speech is divided into segments. Don't worry if a child hears "all of a sudden" as "allova sudden," or hears "ham and eggs" as "hamaneggs," as long as she hears spaces between other words. The child's knowledge of what is and isn't a word will grow slowly, from repeated encounters with words. The child's awareness that writers write with spaces as well as letters will emerge more quickly.

You'll definitely support today's teaching point as you work across the day. In interactive writing (which should be at a time that is totally separate from the writing workshop), after the class has decided what to write, ask them, "How many words is that?" Clap out the number of words or count them out. During reading conferences, say to an individual child, "Can you show me the first word you'll read? Point under it. Show me the next word you'll read." Use the same vocabulary across the day as you support children as they develop a sense of one-to-one matching . . . and the value of white spaces.

When you take your children's work home, you'll probably be pleased to see that they are representing more sounds in their words. On the other hand, it's almost certain that many of your children will have forgotten to write tightly focused Tiny Moment stories. They'll probably be choosing broad topics, and their stories will seem more like lists of everything they did than like stories. This shouldn't surprise you. Throughout the year, you'll find that when you emphasize a new aspect of writing (as you will have done with your new emphasis on conventions), some children will forget all your prior instruction. This is natural, but of course it is not okay because we are teaching for life, and our goal is for instruction to make a lasting impression. In this instance, children will be especially prone to forget concerns over content because a focus on convention is not only *different* from a focus on content, it also *conflicts with* a focus on content. This is why we, as adult writers, often say, when we are drafting, "I'll just spell as best I can for now and come back later to fix it." Of course, a concern for convention will be all the more taxing on a young child, for whom very little has reached the level of automaticity. And so it shouldn't surprise you if your children have focused less on their content and craft now that your teaching has created a new concern for mechanics.

You will want to make note of the fact that your children's progress toward writing well-formed narratives was less stable than you may have thought, but you've still got a lot of time in front of you. For now, you will no doubt want to run back and forth between minilessons that focus on convention and those that focus on content, genre, and qualities of good writing.

CHECKING CONTENT: FOCUSED SMALL MOMENT STORIES

GETTING READY

▶ One child's unfocused story with permission from the writer to take the story apart to help create a Tiny Moment story

● See CD-ROM for resources

WRITING REQUIRES THAT WE BALANCE OUR ATTENTION *between content and convention. The risk in the past few sessions is that we've focused so much on convention that children will forget to write tightly focused, chronological stories and to incorporate story language and story structure into their writing. (See* Small Moments.*) This session attempts to right the imbalance a bit by reminding writers that their content matters, and specifically, by encouraging them to write focused narratives.*

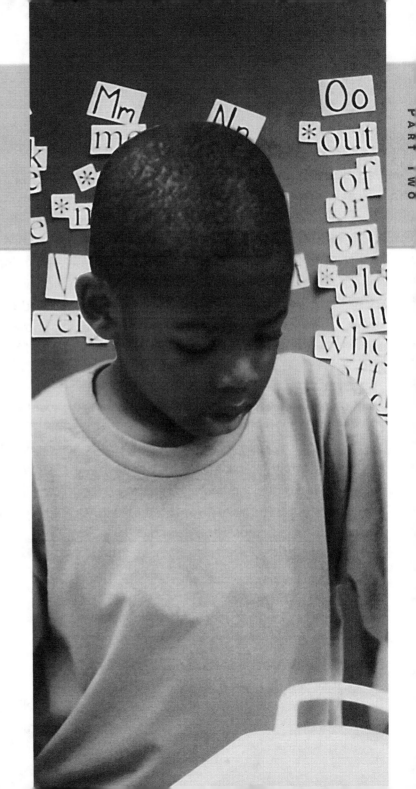

Connection

Tell children that their attention to letters and spaces has made some of them forget all about writing focused Tiny Moment stories.

"Writers, during the past few days we have been making our writing easier to read and that's important. But I have noticed that a lot of you are not writing Tiny Moment stories anymore. You are writing stories that tell a little bit about many, many, many parts of your day. Today, let's remember to write stories that retell *one tiny thing* that happened. We need to remember to hold on to one moment and tell a lot about it. I want to show you one strategy that helped Serena write a Tiny Moment story. I think it could help all of us."

Teaching

Tell the story of one writer who realized her story went on and on, and then fixed it by taking out her staples and choosing one page to become a whole new story.

"Writers, listen to the smart work Serena has done. I have up here the story that Serena wrote. After she wrote her story, Serena reread it and said, 'Wait. It goes on and on about a lot of different things.' Serena thought, 'Hmm. I'm not sure this is a Tiny Moment story.' See if you agree with her," Natalie said and read Serena's book aloud:

> Me and my mom got our lunch.
> Then I got on the swing.
> We got on the bus.

"You know what Serena did next? Can I tell you? She said, 'Wait! I have a lot of *different* stories here!' She realized that almost every page could be grown

Natalie has decided to highlight the importance of focus, not only because this will raise the quality of her students' writing, but also because she is teaching children that her lessons are meant to make a lasting difference and that she doesn't expect them to forget their earlier work just because her teaching shifts to a new concern. Also, she wants to be sure her children always remember that writing involves attention to content and focus and smaller-scale issues, such as white spaces and letters.

Because this unit of study tends to focus on print (and because her children are still beginning writers and tend not to write long pieces), Natalie often recopies her children's writing in enlarged form on chart paper. She didn't need to do so in this instance (the minilesson isn't about the print) but thought it would help her children pay attention. For this situation, there was no need to maintain Serena's approximate spellings.

The verbs in this story aren't very precise. This may be because the author is an English language learner. Such a child will also sometimes have difficulty with prepositions and pronouns, including confusing he *with* she.

The words of this minilesson are illustrated in a very concrete way by the image of a book that goes on and on and on, versus the Tiny Moment story. In teaching young

into a different story. So she took the staples out from her book and said, 'I have three stories, not one story.' She realized she could add onto this page and write a whole story about," Natalie held up page two, "'Then I got on the swing!' She's saving that for later. And she realized she could write a whole story about," Natalie held up page three, "'Me and my mom got on the bus.' Isn't that amazing!"

"So Serena took this one page, 'Me and my mom got our lunch,' and wrote about just that tiny moment. Her Tiny Moment now goes like this:"

My mom and me got our lunch at McDonald's, and I ate french fries, chicken nuggets, and a cheeseburger.

I also got a 101 Dalmatians toy. I press the button on the back, and the dog barks and it crawls.

When he crawls in my pocket, it tickles me.

"Wow! You see how Serena told us details about just the lunch!"

Active Engagement

Tell children to look through their folders for a story that goes on and on and on, like Serena's first story, and then reread it to find one page to turn into a whole book.

"So today and often in your writing lives, I hope you will all look through your folders and see if you have some stories that go on and on and on. If you do, remember that writers sometimes make a whole story out of just one page."

Ask all children to help several children do this, one at a time.

"While we are on the rug, will you help Brian look through his folder? I'll read his pieces, and will you say whether these are on and on and on pieces," Natalie rolled her hand around and around and around like a wheel that turns and turns and turns, "or tiny moments." She cupped her hand. "How 'bout this one?" She read one story and the children called out (and made the accompanying gestures) to indicate that it went on and on and on. "And this one?" She read this one and everyone cupped a hand, agreeing it was a tiny moment. "And this?" They decided it was another on-and-on piece.

children, it is helpful to ask, "What are the big concepts?" and then to find physical, concrete ways to convey those big ideas. The fact that Serena took the staples out of her book and then wrote a new story based on just one page of the original text is a very concrete way to illustrate the concept of focus.

You can also convey the way that some children's stories go on and on and on with an intonation that rolls on, and on, and on, and with hand motions that suggest these stories circle round and round and round endlessly, like a wheel turning and turning. You may want to refer to Tiny Moment stories with cupped hands as if the story fits in the palm of your hand. The physical actions that reinforce meaning are especially important if your class contains many English language learners. You'll especially want to help children comprehend this important instructional language, because understanding this language is necessary to life in the classroom.

You'll want to remind your children to pay attention to the quality of their stories. To do this, you can go back to the Small Moments unit and teach variations of those minilessons. By reminding children to write detailed stories that make sense, you teach children the juggling act of attending to both content and convention—both matter. This is an important tension in writing.

You must also bear in mind that the overall development of writers and their muscles may benefit from a few weeks in which your emphasis (and theirs) is weighted toward convention. This phase will pass. Bear in mind that you can always stop the unit when you think it's time to turn your children's attention back to content.

"I bet Brian will look back at one of his on-and-on-and-on pieces and he'll take just one page and make a whole story out of it. Let me read this again and see if you and a friend could find a way to take one page and make a story out of it." [*Fig. VI-1*]

Link

Suggest that during intervals in their writing work, children might reread to see if their stories go "on and on" and need focus.

"Writers, when you are writing today, finish whatever piece you were working on. Then instead of starting a new one right away, you might decide to go through your own folder and see if you have a story like Brian and Serena had—one that goes on and on. I bet you it'll have a page that could be turned into a whole new story. If you find you have this, remember that writers often decide to write Tiny Moment stories because then we can write with details. When you write Tiny Moment stories, you don't tell about your *whole* trip or *whole* day or *whole* visit, but about one little thing that happened. Writers know readers love to zoom in on the most interesting thing, the most exciting part of the story."

By asking writers to join Brian in rereading several pieces he's written and determining if each piece is or isn't an on-and-on-and-on story, you give children lots of opportunities to apply and practice the lessons you've tried to teach.

Fig. VI-1   Brian

I was skateboarding in the rain and I was going to the train station. I went to the store to buy my hat. I saw my grandmother.

TIME TO CONFER

Even though your minilesson today dealt with focus, much of your conferring will continue to help children who need support writing in ways others can read.

In your conferences, you'll continue to teach writers to listen for sounds in their words, reread as they write, leave spaces between words, and so forth. Teach by demonstrating when this is warranted ("watch me") and by asking the child to do as you've done ("now you try it"). Teach also by coaching into what the child does, remembering to allow approximations and to use lean prompts to lift the level of the child's approximations one tiny step.

In addition to this work with conventions, you'll want a few conferences to focus on the content and structure of children's stories. Keep your eye out for children who are writing Tiny Moments. Your share meeting at the end of this session could be a reading of four or five good examples of Tiny Moment narratives.

Recall the conferences that you held often during the Small Moments unit and be sure to hold a few conferences that help children to focus, to make movies in their mind of what they are describing, to write with detail. See the conferences listed to the right.

Meanwhile, continue to watch for signs of progress. Pay special attention to the errors children make when they spell because these give you windows into the child's logic and intelligence. For example, Brian has written, "I was skateboarding in the rain and I was going to the train station. I went to the store. . . ." [*Fig. VI-1 on previous page*] See if you can discern the logic behind his spelling of in, rain, and store. It should dawn on you that he is over-articulating his final sounds, so that *in* becomes *in-nuh* and *rain* becomes *rain-nuh* and *store*, *stor-ah*—and his spellings match the sounds. You need to know this because the last thing he needs you to do is to encourage him to say the words more slowly, to really stretch them out and to record the sounds.

These conferences in *The Conferring Handbook* may be especially helpful today:

- ▶ *"Say and Record a Word, Then Reread"*
- ▶ *"If You Erase that Word and Scoot It Over, It Will Be Easier to Read"*
- ▶ *"Famous Writers Use Periods to Tell Readers When to Stop"*

Also, if you have *Conferring with Primary Writers*, you may want to refer to the following conferences:

- ▶ "Can You Reenact That Part in a Way That Shows Me Exactly What Happened?"
- ▶ "What Is the Most Important Part of Your Story?"

Read and bask in a few examples of Tiny Moment narratives written by your children.

"Okay, everyone, I am just going to read to you some examples of Tiny Moment stories that different writers in this class have done. I want you to notice how in every one, the writer tried hard to tell something very interesting about their moment. None of these stories tell just a little about lots of different moments. They tell a lot about just one moment. That is the kind of story you should all be writing during the next few weeks." [*Figs. VI-2, VI-3, and VI-4*]

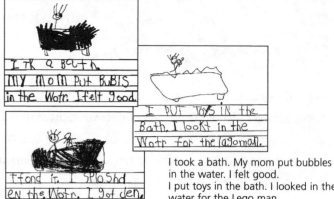

I took a bath. My mom put bubbles in the water. I felt good.
I put toys in the bath. I looked in the water for the Lego man.
I found it. I splashed in the water. I got clean.

Fig. VI-2   Kayla

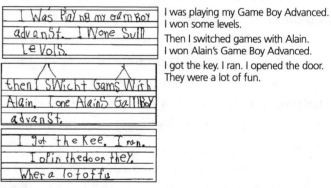

I was playing my Game Boy Advanced. I won some levels.

Then I switched games with Alain. I won Alain's Game Boy Advanced.

I got the key. I ran. I opened the door. They were a lot of fun.

Fig. VI-3   Jesus

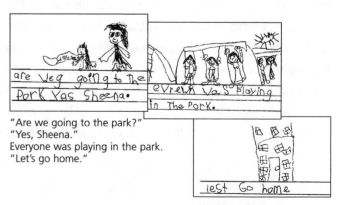

"Are we going to the park?"
"Yes, Sheena."
Everyone was playing in the park.
"Let's go home."

Fig. VI-4   Sheena

LEARNING MORE SIGHT WORDS

GETTING READY

- Check writing paper supply
- Make sure children have writing folders with them
- Provide a set of wipe-off boards, markers, and an eraser (a sock) for every child (or, if necessary, every pair of children)
- See CD-ROM for resources

IT IS IMPORTANT FOR CHILDREN TO DEVELOP *a repertoire of words they can spell and read without applying any word-solving strategies. Researcher Sandra Wilde found that half the words our children read and write are the same thirty-six words. Most children will learn these words from many encounters with them, but we can hasten this process by teaching some of these words directly. You'll probably devote twenty minutes each day to word study, and you'll probably use a portion of this time to teach children new high frequency words. If you teach a few new high frequency words each week during word study time, you can then devote some minilessons to teaching children that writers use the high frequency words they already know to help them tackle unfamiliar words. Teach children that if they know* like, *they can easily write* bike.

Many high frequency or "word-wall" words give writers the word-power to read and write other *words.*

Preface all of this instruction with, "I noticed many of you are having some trouble writing the word _____" so that your children know spelling matters for one big reason: we need to spell words so people can read our writing.

In this session, you'll remind children that they can write some words in a snap, without sounding them out. You'll teach a new word they'll now know in a snap, and remind them to use the word wall when they write.

THE MINILESSON

Connection

Celebrate that the class has been writing Tiny Moments that *you can read*. Then tell them that today, you'll make the work a bit easier and faster.

"It was wonderful to read your Tiny Moments yesterday. Two things were wonderful. First, I loved that so many of you are writing with details about tiny moments. And second, I love that more and more, I can read your great stories! You've been working hard to listen to and sound out words. It's been hard and slow work. Today I want to remind you that we each have words we know in a snap. These words make writing a lot easier and faster."

Teaching

Tell children that while it's great that they listen carefully to the sounds in some words, they need to have other words they can spell quickly. Show them that they already know a few words well.

"I have noticed that when you all are writing, you very often spell words by listening carefully to the sounds in the words. This is one good way to write a word. The great news, though, is that each of you has a pocketful of words you know by heart, and those words are a snap for you to write. Pretend you have paper in front of you. On your pretend paper (really on the carpet), write *me*." They did. "You know what? I didn't see any of you sounding it out. You just said, '*Me*, I know *me*,' and you wrote it in a snap. Try *Mom*." They did. "Again—snap! You just knew it."

Teach children one new sight word. Give them the word and ask them to say what they notice about it.

"Today I want to teach you a word I think *will* come in real handy for you. It is *will*. We use *will* when we talk about what we *will* do next, after this, in the future. We *will* go to lunch later. We *will* have recess. And soon, we *will* learn to spell *will*. Let me write it for you." I did. "As you know, whenever we try to

Notice that I'm returning to a phrase I used early in this unit of study when I mentioned in passing that there are some words kids know in a snap. There are a vast number of instructional words that children need to learn to succeed in school, and we do children a favor if we don't use too many synonyms. If you once spoke of high frequency words as "words we know in a snap," you will want to return to this descriptor again and again. Make physical motions to accompany the expression and you'll help all your children and especially your English language learners.

I am about to teach children something new, and I know that before moving to new terrain, it can help to consolidate the fact that there are items similar to the new item that they already know. You remind them that they have a great track record as learners-of-words. You help them approach the new work with a sense of "this will be easy for me."

learn a new word, we first study it, so let's do that now. Look at *will* and tell someone near you what you notice." They talked. "What are you noticing?"

"It starts with a *w*. Not that many words do."

"It gots two short letters and two tall guys."

"All the letters are sticks not tunnels and circles."

Ask children to take a mental picture of the new word.

"Good noticing. Let's look at the word as if our minds were cameras and try to take a mental picture of it." Pretending to hold a camera, I pointed to the word, and said, "Click. Take a picture in your mind so you remember it for always."

Ask children to write the word on their wipe boards.

Now, covering the word, I said, "Can you see it in your mind? Try to. Try writing it on your wipe board." They did. "Check it and study it again. Take another picture of it in your mind." Again I covered the word. "Write it on your board again—write it fast." They did. "Check it."

"When you go home and you are almost asleep and you think, '*Will . . .*' will you remember it? Next week, will it still be stuck in your head like glue?"

Active Engagement

Tell writers you'll now put the new word on the word wall. Remind them of how it'll give them word power.

"Writers, now that you know *will*, I'm going to put it up on our word wall. And knowing this word should help you with a lot of words. If you want to write, 'I *will* have a play date,' how will you spell *will*—I *will* have a play date? (w-i-l-l)."

"Here is the hard question. How will this word help with this sentence? 'I hold still when he cuts my hair.' Tell your friend. How 'bout in *this* sentence? 'It is a chilly day.' Tell your friend."

Children will use the terms you've taught them to say what they see. This child talks of tunnels and circles because the class has sorted magnetic letters into letters with circles (a, b, d, g, p, q), with tunnels (u, n, m, h), with dots (i, j) and crosses (x, t, f).

Just as children say words they've heard you say, we, too, pick up the language of our colleagues. In this minilesson, I've incorporated some of researcher Diane Snowball's ways of helping children learn a new sight word. Don't hesitate to borrow from every source imaginable when you teach children (and to acknowledge your sources when you talk or write to other teachers).

This last extension makes your minilesson more multilevel.

Link

Remind children that if they forget the word, they need to study it on the word wall, to take a mental picture.

"Writers, if you want to write to my friend *William* and you forget how to spell *will*, look up here on the word wall. But don't copy the letters! That won't help you! Instead, if you forget the word, look at the word again. Notice how the word looks. Get a new picture in your mind. Then, write it on your paper and check if it's okay, just like we did today."

MID-WORKSHOP TEACHING POINT

Tell about a child who was stretching out a word and realized, instead, that he knew a chunk of it.

"I want to show you the coolest thing. Christopher was writing *become* and he said, 'I don't know that word.' Then he started to stretch it out slowly and he said, 'Wait! *Be* . . . I know *be,*' and he wrote be in a snap. Then he reread it '*be*' and said '*become*' and he started to sound out come when he said, 'Wait, I think I know *come.*' He wasn't quite sure so he found it on the word wall, studied it, took a picture of it with his mind, and soon he'd written *become*."

Remind children that the words they know can give them word power.

"I hope all of you are learning that the words you know can give you word power. Let's try it. Pretend you wanted to write 'I feel *glad*.' Which word do you know that can help you with *glad*? (Dad.) Pretend you want to write 'I ate *meat*,' which word can help with *meat*? (Me). Don't forget, if you aren't sure how to spell a word, let the words you know give you word power."

When you teach children a new high frequency word, you are teaching them a process for imprinting new words onto their brain. For this reason, it is wise to progress through the same sequence of steps with each new high frequency word. Once children have taken a mental picture of lots of high frequency words, they should be able to do this on their own.

Notice that the minilessons in this unit build on each other. In the early minilessons, children stretched words out and heard dominant sounds. Now you show that children can also hear chunks of words. The changes in your message reflect children's progress, and they also suggest that at the start of a unit you tailor your teaching to children with the greatest needs. Later you aim your teaching at higher levels.

TIME TO CONFER

Although usually you won't align all your conferences with that day's minilesson, in this unit of study you will often do this.

You may want to say, "I'm admiring the way you use the words you know to spell new words." Carry a clipboard and act ready to record whatever they do. The kids will perform on cue. As you watch, you'll probably see kids copy words from the word wall. When you see this, teach them to study the word, to articulate what they notice about it, to take a mental picture of it, then to write it without copying it and to later double-check themselves. You'll want to remind them that many—even most—of the words they want to write contain chunks that are in the word-wall words. If a child goes to write strike, say, "You already know strike because there's a word like it on the word wall."

Remember that good spellers do not spell most words by sounding them out! Instead, they rely on a variety of strategies. The strategy you've highlighted in this session is only one in a writer's repertoire. Therefore, when you help children with spelling, instead of making a habit of only saying, "What sounds do you hear?" you'll want to nudge writers to use all the strategies available to them. Ask "Did you try that word? Which strategy did you use?"

While you support your children's use of high frequency words, remember that your teaching needs to keep all your goals alive. Use the conferring checklist to remind you of goals for your teaching.

These conferences in *The Conferring Handbook* may be especially helpful today:

- ▶ *"Say and Record a Word, Then Reread"*
- ▶ *"If You Erase That Word and Scoot It Over, It Will Be Easier to Read"*
- ▶ *"Famous Writers Use Periods to Tell Readers Where to Stop"*

Also, if you have *Conferring with Primary Writers*, you may want to refer to the conferences in part three.

AFTER-THE-WORKSHOP SHARE

Ask children to sort their writing into hard-to-read and easy-to-read piles. Ask them to make the easy pile even easier to read.

"Writers, we've been doing a lot of work to make sure readers can read our stories. Earlier you made two piles—a hard-to-read and an easier-to-read pile. Today will you go through your writing and again put it in two piles—a hard-to-read and an easier-to-read pile. Then try to read the pieces in the easier-to-read pile. Read with your pen in your hand and if you find things that need fixing, fix them."

USING PERSONAL WORD WALLS

GETTING READY

▶ Copies of your classroom's word wall duplicated so that each child can receive a personal copy

▶ Plastic sleeves that are the right size to hold the word walls. Each child needs his or her own plastic word-wall sleeve, and these need to be kept in the child's writing folder. You may also add a word wall chart into the plastic sleeve on the back of the child's wipe board

▶ Children will need their writing folders with them

● See CD-ROM for resources

BECAUSE WE VERY MUCH WANT CHILDREN *to rely on high frequency words when they write, it makes sense to give each child a personalized copy of the word wall. In most classrooms, we give children a plastic casing with a copy of that week's word wall slid into it. This way, every week or so, we can update their personalized word walls to match the word wall on the classroom wall.*

In every unit of study, we try to give children a new tool or two that helps to carry the message of that unit. Tools can do a great deal to create identities. When I resolve to begin jogging, it helps me to purchase a new jogging suit. "Why do you need this?" my husband asks, "you don't jog." I tell him that first I need the suit, then I'll remake myself to match the outfit! Children, too, first begin to carry around a new tool and then grow into the identities of being the kinds of people who need that new tool.

In this session, you'll teach your children to use their individual copies of the word wall as a resource when they write.

The Minilesson

Connection

Give children an example of using one word to spell many using a word they learned in the last session.

"Last time you learned how to spell *will* and we put it on our word wall. When you know *will*, it can help you write a sign saying, 'Do not . . . spill!' Start, in your mind, with the word *will*. Can you see it? Write *will* with your finger on the carpet. Now, with a make believe eraser, take away the /w/ from *will* and what do you have? ill. So now, on the carpet, turn your *ill* into *spill*. (I did it on chart paper.) Now, let's say you ran up the *hill* to dry your *spill*. Take the /sp/ from *spill* (on the carpet) and turn *ill* into *hill*. So you see, if we know a word, this gives you a lot of word power. Today, we'll learn more about using word power when we write."

"I'm going to give each one of you your own personal copy of our word wall. Today I want to show you how word-wall words can give you word power whenever you write."

It's a great thing when some of your minilessons fit tongue-and-groove into each other, as this one does with the one that preceded it.

It will help if you are doing this sort of making-word work during word study time.

Teaching

Show children that words are categorized on the word wall according to their first letter. Have children find a word or two on their personal word walls by first deciding what letter the word begins with.

"Now that you each have your own personal word wall, I want you to notice that your personal word walls have the exact same words that you'll see on our classroom word wall. The words are organized under their starting letter. So, if I wanted to find the word *me*, I'd look under *m*. See if you can find *me* on your word walls with your finger." They did.

"Good. Each word is written under the letter it begins with."

You may think all your children know how to find words on the word wall, but don't be so sure! This is crucial enough that you'll want to teach it explicitly. I begin with the word me *because it is especially accessible, and I want all children to have early success finding words on the word wall. Function words are more challenging than nouns and pronouns, which have more concrete meanings.*

"Now what if I was writing a story about skateboarding *down* the ramp, but I wasn't sure about *down, /d/own*? Which letter would you go to?"

"D."

"Is it there? Point to it with your finger."

Once they've found a word, show children how to learn from (rather than copy from) the word wall.

"If you wanted to put *down* in your story, first you need to look at the word and say, in your head or to a friend, what you notice. Do that now (in your heads). Then you need to look at the word and take a mental picture of it. Study it. Try to get it into your mind. Close your eyes and try to see *down*. Now check what you remembered with the word wall. Study it again."

Active Engagement

Have the children practice using the word wall in service of their writing,

"Okay everyone, right now will you try using your word walls while you sit here on the carpet? Get out yesterday's story and start to add on to it right here. Like always, first reread what you already wrote and think, 'What will I say next?' Then you start to write. As you write, say each word to yourself and think, 'Do I know that word? If you know it in a snap, put it down. If you *almost* know how it goes but you aren't sure, it's probably on the word wall, so find the word. Study it. Take a picture of it with your mind. Then look away from the word wall and write it on your paper."

You'll notice that our minilessons often repeat whatever we taught the day before. You are recycling this same lesson often.

It is wise to have children reread what they've written and begin adding onto it before they refer to the word wall. This will make it unlikely that the word wall determines the content of their writing. You don't want a list of words to influence the content of your children's writing! Sometimes a few children see the word wall as a way to write without having to sound out so many words—which in a way it is—but these writers can get into some trouble if they end up basing their ideas for stories on the words that happen to be on the word wall!

Link

Remind children that writers first have stories in mind and only then use the word wall as a reference. Stories aren't written by stringing together words from the word wall.

"Let me ask you something, would this be a good way to write?" I looked at the board and touched some words saying, as I did, a sentence that strung those words together: "He have a good and happy. . . ."

"No!"

"Right, just like before, you will begin with the story in your mind that you want to tell other people. The story you have to tell is not on your word walls. Get out yesterday's writing and remember what you want to say and keep going, but have your word walls close on hand."

If you don't want your kids to do something—out with it! We need to get better at being explicit and straightforward. Notice that instead of talking about the fact that it's not wise to write by stringing together known words, I reenact this and do so in a way that makes such a process seem a bit silly.

TIME TO CONFER

Be on the lookout for children who rely on the word wall as a source for all their words. This can turn writing into a word-combining exercise. When you come upon a child who is using his personal word wall in this way, you need to steer this word-wall copier back to her own voice and her own stories. Help this child to draw with detail and to tell a story, touching the pages on which the child plans to write. Stay with this child until she can use the word wall as support and not as a source.

On the other hand, you will also want to watch for children who are not taking the time to spell words they almost know correctly. You could always highlight the spellings of these words by suggesting that once a writer has learned a word such as *with*, that writer would profit from rereading old pieces the writer has written, looking for other times he used *with* and fixing it every time. This provides the child with lots of practice with a word the child almost knows.

Remember that the work you have done all year encouraging children to write Small Moments needs to be kept alive in your conferences. It is crucial for children to understand that word walls and spelling patterns are simply tools to be used in the service of writing and sharing grand stories. Among other things, be sure that at least one of your conferences, like those listed to the right, helps writers focus their stories. All the conferences that were crucial in the *Small Moments* unit can continue as mainstays now.

These conferences in *The Conferring Handbook* may be especially helpful today:

- ▶ *"Say and Record a Word, Then Reread"*
- ▶ *"If You Erase That Word and Scoot It Over, It Will Be Easier to Read"*
- ▶ *"Famous Writers Use Periods to Tell Readers Where to Stop"*

Also, if you have *Conferring with Primary Writers*, you may want to refer to the conferences in part three.

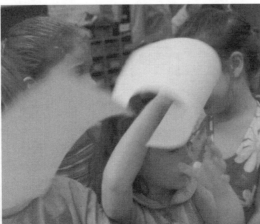

Celebrate a child who has invented an interesting thing to do with his or her word wall. In this instance, Natalie tells the class that she found a child trying to read with her word wall chart.

"Today I saw Ana doing the most amazing thing. She thought it up all by herself. Right, Ana?" This was Ana's first year in this country and she was learning English fast.

"Ana was reading her personal word wall. She said, 'I want to see if I know all these words.' Sometimes, she came to a word she'd forgotten and she checked it with me. Soon, she really had all those word wall words in her mind! Because she'd done that, it helped her writing! Later, she needed to write the word *and*. She started to sound it out but then she said, 'I think *and* is on my sheet. I remember it.' She knew because she's read her sheet! Then later in the same story, her word wall helped her again. Ana needed to write *hand*. She used what she knew about and to help her figure out how to write *hand*." [*Fig. VIII-1*]

Ask the class to follow the example and reread their word walls with a friend.

"Right now, will you work together with a friend and try to use Ana's idea. Reread your personal word walls. I think this will help us all remember words that we almost know by heart—and it'll remind you which words are on your list, too."

Fig. VIII-1   Ana

Me and my family went to the
park. We saw a snowman.
He almost fell. My dad held
his hand.

▸ For more practice, this session's minilesson can be adapted and done again many times or turned into small group strategy lessons. You could remind writers to rely on their knowledge of some words on the run as they write sentences by writing sentences publicly using a range of strategies. For example, you might say, "Watch how I use all these strategies on the chart to write a sentence," and then, for active involvement, you might say something like, "Let's work with our friends and try writing a sentence. See if you can remember to do all these things. Let's pretend you are writing about Sebastian's birthday and you wanted to write, 'We will eat Sebastian's birthday cake.' Use strategies to help yourself write that on your white boards and I'll admire what you do."

▸ If you notice the wise innovations your kids make on the whole concept of word walls their innovations can become the grounds for minilessons. Natalie and I noticed, for example, that a handful of writers used their word walls as resources when they reread their pieces. They'd read along, get to a place where they were unsure of the spelling, check their spellings against those on the word wall, and then change the word as needed. When we saw this, we know we'd celebrate it in a minilesson. We want all children to know that the word walls could be a tool not only during writing, but also during editing, and we want children to be encouraged to invent their own wonderful ideas.

Take home and look at every piece of writing that every child has written. For now, pay attention to volume as well as to the quality of the writing. Usually this reality check is a bit depressing. Most of us go through thinking, "Nothing that I teach is having an impact." The truth is, growth is slow and involves two steps forward and one step backwards. This is especially true when the areas for growth are as complex as those your children are encountering.

Pay attention to your children's writing even when what you see is discouraging. Natalie and I found, at this point in her unit, that quite a few of her children were no longer writing focused narratives. Focusing on convention took a bigger toll on the children's narratives than we'd expected. For some of her children, we accepted writing that was unfocused and lacking in detail for now because meanwhile, the progress these children were making on matters like leaving white space, recording dominant sounds in words, and spelling high frequency words correctly was impressive.

Some children were producing less writing than we expected, and this was an issue we *didn't* want to skirt. While we were sure that production had slowed because children were working to hear more sounds, the writers had slowed down too much. Natalie would talk with them about finding a balance between making sure people can read our writing and pushing ourselves to get more of our ideas onto paper.

Try to decide whether most of the children are writing in ways that *you* and also *they* can read. You will want to raise the ante around convention soon and before you can proceed, double check that you won't ask too much of children.

WRITING MORE, AND MORE CLEARLY

GETTING READY

▶ Three- or four-page writing booklets with the date and each child's name

◉ See CD-ROM for resources

NATALIE AND I EMERGED FROM OUR ASSESSMENTS *determined to emphasize that quantity counts. You will find your own priorities in the particulars of your children's work. If you teach a specific unit of study several years in a row (as most of us do), each time you teach the unit, your teaching may begin similarly, but the work that comes midway into the unit will be influenced by whatever you see when you study your children. With this particular class, for example, we needed to emphasize* volume *of writing. With other classes, the issues may be different.*

Natalie knew from her earlier work with Tiny Moments that most of her writers were capable of writing one story each day, assuming a story was three stapled-together pages, each with a picture and two or three sentences. To Natalie's dismay, production during this unit had slowed down so that some children were writing closer to one story per week! To encourage production from all of the writers in her class, Natalie decided to take a little more control of writing workshop than she usually took. She decided to emphasize the importance of volume and stamina by instituting a short-term policy of asking each child to start and finish a new story each day.

In this session, you'll increase your writers' productivity by suggesting that as a short term measure, they aim to begin and end a new story each day, writing across three or four pages.

THE MINILESSON

Connection

Tell children that studying their writing helped you realize they needed not only to continue to make their writing easier to read, but that they also needed to write more.

"Everyone, yesterday after we used our word walls, I took every one of your folders home. I loaded them in my bag and I couldn't wait to get home to read your amazing stories. I was ready for a night filled with six, seven, or eight stories from each of you. It was going to be a great night, filled with a lot of reading of all of your stories! But, you know what happened? I started to read through your folders and then, I was done. Just like that!"

"I could see that you all have worked hard to make your stories easier to read, and almost every story I brought home was easy to read, but there weren't that many stories! Some of you only had three stories in your folder! From today on, I want you to keep writing in ways that are easy to understand, but I also want you *to write more.*"

Teaching

Let children know that to get better as writers they need to write a lot. Tell them for a few days you will help them keep track of how much writing they get done each day.

"Writers, it is so important that you push yourselves to write as much as you can. It's important to write in a way that's easy to read, but it is also important to write a lot."

"So writing workshop will be a little different for the rest of the week. For the next few days, I am going to keep your folders, and each day, I am going to give you a booklet that has that day's date on it. You will get a booklet today with today's date on it. Then tomorrow, you will get *another* three-page booklet with *tomorrow's* date on it. The challenge will be: can you write a story a day for the next three days, and can you still write easy-to-read stories? You'll need to push yourselves. Try hard."

I love the bluntness, clarity, and humor of this connection. We do our children no favors to gloss over the problems we see. How wise to blow the whistle, to say, "This has to stop."

This connection is a bit unusual. By the end of the connection, Natalie hasn't told the children what it is she will teach them that she hopes will influence her children's writing always. She's using this minilesson to institute a temporary structure—one that she hopes will have lasting benefits. The connection phase in this minilesson is an effective one, but it is more a vehicle for making an assignment than usual.

Again, this teaching component is not like most. Natalie is telling her children what she wants them to do more than she is teaching them a strategy. This is unusual. It is important for all of us, as teachers, to realize that there will be times when we don't follow our own guidelines for minilessons.

Active Engagement

Ask children to picture the story they want to tell. Ask them to touch each page of their booklet and say aloud the exact story they plan to put on the pages.

"To have more time for actually writing, let's get ourselves ready to write before we leave the rug. Close your eyes and picture the tiny story you want to write today. Picture it in your mind like a movie. Now, I want you to touch each page of your booklet and say aloud to yourselves the part of the story that will go on that page. When you have done this, close your story pages and look up at me."

Link

Tell the children that for the next few days they will use the time on the rug to get themselves ready to do *a lot* of easy-to-read writing.

"We'll do this every day for the next few days. We'll plan our stories on the rug so we can get started right away. You are going to try to write a whole story today—and an easy-to-read story. I will remind you of how much time has gone by throughout the workshop."

Notice that this active involvement is not a traditional one either. Because Natalie hasn't exactly taught a skill or strategy, her kids can't practice that skill or strategy now.

As you confer, keep an eye on your children's productivity. Who gets started right away and who doesn't? Notice your children's stamina as writers and prepare to move children to their own private writer's desks if they need solitude to have staying power. Are some of them drawing with too much detail rather than sketching? Do some of them sit paralyzed with indecision when confronting difficulty? Do some of them seem to wait for you to come around and give them a personal jump-start? Respond to the problems you see either in conferences or by convening a small group of children who require similar instruction.

If you feel as if some children need to be reminded of the expectations during a writing workshop, refer to "Where Is Your Writing Work?" and "Writers Share Community Supplies." as models for holding children accountable to working hard.

Meanwhile, use your conferring guidelines and notice what children seem to be able to do on their own. Notice also what they still need to learn, and use conferring as a time for intense instruction.

These conferences in *The Conferring Handbook* may be especially helpful today:

▶ *"Say and Record a Word, Then Reread"*

▶ *"If You Erase That Word and Scoot It Over, It Will Be Easier to Read"*

▶ *"Famous Writers Use Periods to Tell Readers Where to Stop"*

Also, if you have *Conferring with Primary Writers*, you may want to refer to the following conferences:

▶ "Where Is Your Writing Work?"

▶ "Writers Share Community Supplies"

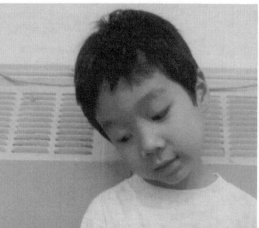

AFTER-THE-WORKSHOP SHARE

Tell children that you want them to bring today's writing to the carpet. Ask them to make a pile of finished stories for you to read tonight, and another pile of not-finished stories that will sit in the room.

"Okay, all of you, bring your writing to the carpet. In a moment, we're going to make a pile of finished stories from today that I can take home tonight to read. Everyone who has a finished story, would you come up and put it in the middle of the circle now? (Don't direct them. Let them decide for themselves if their story is finished.) People with stories still needing more work, leave them in this bin. Finally, everyone who feels like they made their writing easier to read, could you raise your hand. Hurrah! If you feel as if you wrote as much as you could today, raise your hand. Okay, great. Tomorrow we will pay more attention to these two things."

In an understated way, Natalie lets children know that there are rewards for finishing a story. The reward for these young writers and for any writer is the thrill of having readers.

Today's lesson will mean nothing if you don't take a quick look tonight at the pile of finished stories. If the story is in the finished pile, does it have a picture and at least a sentence on each page? Was the writing easy to read? Did it show any evidence of having been reread by the author?

Look also at the stories in the not-finished pile. What information do you have to help you understand why these writers did not finish? Is this one a talker instead of a writer? Could it be this writer was so fixated on writing readable words that he or she wrote only a few words? Try to understand the true story of your classroom. Record what you notice and be sure, tomorrow, to speak with children who put not-done stories in the finished-work pile. Help them begin tomorrow with new resolve.

Before today's minilesson, Brian had written this during one day. [*Fig. IX-1*]

I watched while he wrote this, and could see he was becoming obsessed with the correctness of his writing. I also knew, from the detail in his pictures, that he had much more story hidden in him. (Note the hilarious scribble scrabble at the bottom of the picture on page three. That's Natalie's messy closet from which she got the tooth bag.) I wanted to nudge this obviously detail-oriented writer back to his storytelling. On the day of this minilesson he wrote this. [*Fig. IX-2*]

This was Brian, the storyteller, back to balancing fluency and accuracy!

Fig. IX-I   Brian

Yesterday my tooth came out.
And I told my [teacher] they came out.
Then the teacher gave me a bag to put my tooth [in].

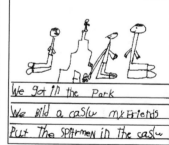

I was going to the park with my friends and when we got there I said, "Can we make a castle?"
We got in the park. We build a castle. My friends put the Spidermen in the castle.
When my friends put the Spidermen in the castle, the Spidermen knocked down the castle. I said, "Can we leave because I am cold?" And we left.

Fig. IX-2   Brian

WRITING FOR PARTNERS

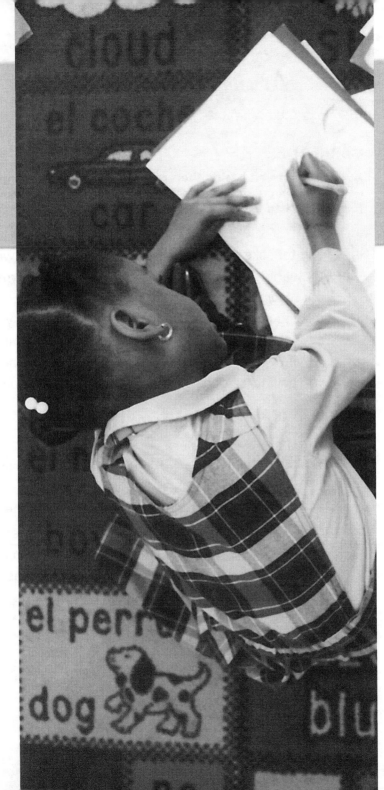

GETTING READY

▶ Each child's writing from last session and a new story booklet for each child with that child's name and the date written on it. Have these sitting at each child's desk.

▶ Your own story written on a chart paper booklet. Be sure your writing is dark enough and large enough for your writers to read it from their rug spots.

◉ See CD-ROM for resources

THIS SESSION MARKS AN IMPORTANT CHANGE *in the direction of the unit. For a while now, children have tried to write in such a way that we can read their writing. Now we'll ask them to write in such a way that their peers can read what they've written. This is a big step. It's easier for an adult to use the information a child gives and to infer what the child was trying to say than it is for another child to do these things. Asking children to read each other's writing may leave some children feeling dejected that their classmates can't read their writing. But there are tremendous gains to be had from nudging children to write so their classmates can read their writing. Imagine the hard, constructive work of a child adding more and more letters to a word, then passing it to his friend saying, "Now can you read it?" Perhaps in the end, the writer resorts to saying, "I'm trying to say . . ." and then asking his or her friend, "Will you help me write it so you can read it?"*

This session's first partnership minilesson occupies the time slot traditionally reserved for minilessons, but soon our partnership minilessons will be moved to the end of writing time so they directly precede the partnership work. The message is, "Today as you write, remember you are writing for a friend who will try to read your work." We felt sure that if children tried to write for a partner-reader, this would make writing readable drafts into an even more palpable and urgent goal.

THE MINILESSON

Connection

Ask children to sit beside their reading partners. Tell them that today you'll give them help in writing a lot and in writing stories people can read. The help will come in the form of a partner.

"Okay guys, we have been trying our hardest to write as much as we can and to make our writing easy to read. Today you will have a partner help you do these things. Your partners will be *reading* your writing, so I figured why not use our *reading* partnerships. So right now, will you get up and stand beside your reading partner? Now sit down. The place where you are sitting will be your new rug spot. Every day, when you gather for a minilesson or share in the writing workshop, you'll sit here beside your partner. Today I am going to teach you how to be good *writing* partners for each other."

Teaching

Tell the children that being a writing partner is a big responsibility.

"Everyone, it is exciting to have someone look at your writing every day because your partner can help you make your writing better. But having a reader can also be a little scary. I have had writing partners, and they have been both exciting and scary. Because we, as writers, care so much about our stories and try so hard to write them well, our feelings are easily hurt. A good writing partner is someone who helps to make our writing easier to read and someone who takes care of our feelings. Being a writing partner is an important job and you need to do the job carefully."

Logistics matter, and this is nicely streamlined. Get rid of as many logistical problems as possible before you get into the meat of your minilessons.

In the reading workshop, Natalie's children were paired into ability-based partnerships (children often read the same book together). Although our writing partnerships tend not to be ability based, we figured more experienced readers would be more able to read the longer, more complex texts of more experienced writers. We brought the reading partnerships into the writing workshop and also encouraged children to read each other's writing using all the strategies they used to read books.

A lot of good teaching grows out of empathy. Natalie has put herself in her kids' shoes and imagined how this work might feel for them, and her teaching is on the mark because of her empathy.

You'll notice that she acts as if it's a whole new thing for these kids to have writing partnerships, even though the truth is they had a different version of partners earlier in the year.

Recruit all the children to be your partner. This will give them practice as partners.

"So, to help you learn to do this, I am going to have all of you be my writing partner. I have a story up here that I wrote, and I want you to act like my writing partner. Remember that you need to help me make my writing better, *and* you need to take care of my feelings."

Ask them to respond to your illegible writing.

"Okay writers, what do you think of the first page of my story?" (It has no spaces and is very hard to read.)

Stephen shouts out, "I can't read it! There's no spaces!"

If the child responds by saying, "I can't read it!" coach the child to be gentle with your feelings. Give your critic some possible words.

"Stephen, you said something that might remind me to make my writing easier to read, and that's helpful, but my feelings are a little hurt. Can anyone think of a way to tell me that my writing needs spaces while still taking care of my feelings?"

The room was silent. Natalie whispered to Stephen, "Tell me how much you really want to read my story. Then tell me that because there are no spaces, you really can't read it that easily. Say that."

Stephen repeated out loud what Natalie told him to say.

Receiving Stephen's feedback with warm receptivity, Natalie said, "Thanks, Stephen. I'll work on my spaces. My feelings are not hurt now."

Active Engagement

Ask all children to pretend they couldn't read their partner's writing and to tell their partner this nicely.

Then, turning to the class, Natalie said, "Can you all practice saying that same thing about spaces to your partner sitting next to you? Pretend you had trouble reading your partner's writing and tell your partner so. Don't forget to take care of your partners feelings when you talk."

This is an unusual way to do the teaching component of a minilesson. Natalie hasn't explicitly named the strategies she wants her children to use. It would be more typical for us to demonstrate to children what good partners do (perhaps contrasting not-so-good and great partners) and then to tell children what we hope they will do when they act as partners for other writers. But Natalie decides instead to elicit their best effort at being good partners, and in this way to do some public coaching.

It will never be possible to package life in any classroom so there aren't problems. Natalie is fearless in her willingness to confront the issues. Her teaching goes straight to the middle of any problem, and in direct ways, she sets out to make a difference. She carries an absolute conviction that people—even very young and vulnerable kids—can learn, learn, learn.

It's just fine to put words into our kid's mouths. After all, this whole series of books gives you words that you can try on. You'll make them your own in no time. Kids benefit from similar help.

The children all essentially repeated what Stephen said to their own partners.

Link

Remind children that today and always, when they share their writing with a friend, they should help make the writing better *and* take care of their friend's feelings.

"Okay all of you, whenever you work with a writing partner, remember to make your partners' writing easier to read *and* to take care of their feelings. Talk to your partner about how much you want to read their story. For now, let's do our writing—remembering that later your partner will try to read what you wrote today. Before you go, let me give you a new booklet and will you get here on the rug and think about what you'll write today. Tell your story across the pages. Okay, thumbs up when you are ready to start. Off you go."

MID-WORKSHOP TEACHING POINT

Convene your writers and ask them to decide who'll share first. This will be partner one.

"Writers, it's time for our partnership shares. Will you first come back to the meeting area, bring today's writing, and sit with your partner?" They did. "Now partners need to talk and decide who's writing we'll read first." They did. "Okay, the writers of these pieces, you are partner one for today and every day. Thumbs up." They did.

Teach partner one how to share his or her writing. The two children need to point under words, with the writer fixing things if necessary.

"Partner one, would you put your writing between you and partner two. Hold it like you were holding a book. First, the writer needs to talk about the picture. Then the two of you need to point under the words and read the writing together. If you have trouble, maybe the writer can add some letters to make the story easier to read. Then turn the page, and the writer talks about the picture, and you both point under the words. Remember, partner two, your job is to help the writing and take care of the writer's feelings."

When my son is tutored in Spanish, he fumbles to say something. His tutor says the phrase correctly and then says to him, "Say it. Repeat it." I listen to Miles rehearsing his lines, and marvel that good teaching is good teaching. Miles may be learning Spanish and Natalie's children may be learning the language of writing workshops, but for all of us, it helps to try out new ways with words.

Notice that Natalie returns to the phrases she used at the start of the minilesson. She doesn't search for synonyms so that she has an original, new way to phrase her advice. Instead, she repeats this advice often, hoping that in this way her children will internalize the suggestion.

When children sit on the rug in partnerships, you want to be able to ask them to do something and to know they can immediately try what you suggest. If you say, "Help each other with . . ." children might spend two minutes deciding which child shares his or her writing first. The problem is, the entire activity lasts little more than two minutes. If children know they are either partner one or partner two, you can bypass this impasse by saying, "Partner one, listen to partner two's story and. . . ."

TIME TO CONFER

For part of this session, you'll confer to support the partnerships. Observe the partnership (stay back a bit) before intervening to talk about what you see as working and not working. After you make a suggestion, pull back so the partners can try again with your input guiding them.

Try to glean a sense for your children's overall abilities as writing partners. Keep in mind that after that the first day or two of this work, most of us will be tempted to give up on the idea of partnerships. That's normal. Don't give up! But don't assume these relationships are all rosy either. You'll need to see and address problems. If children are unkind to each other, your efforts to make their writing easier to read will be derailed by interpersonal problems. Learning to work well with other people is as valuable as any other lesson your children learn. Children tend to want to make these partnerships work well because they really want other people to hear their stories. They are willing to work very hard to get along so that someone will hear what they have to say. So, even if your children are not very good at these conversations, talk as if the partnerships are amazing and meanwhile, teach hard to improve whatever is less than amazing.

These conferences in *The Conferring Handbook* may be especially helpful today:

▶ *"Say and Record a Word, Then Reread"*

▶ *"If You Erase That Word and Scoot It Over, It Will Be Easier to Read"*

▶ *"Famous Writers Use Periods to Tell Readers Where to Stop"*

Also, if you have *Conferring with Primary Writers*, you may want to refer to the conferences in part three.

After-the-Workshop Share

Share some examples of partnerships working well.

"Oh my gosh, everyone. During your partnership work today, I saw the most amazing things! I saw *everyone* trying their hardest to make their partner's writing easier to read and *everyone* trying their hardest to make sure that they took care of their partner's feelings! Shawn and Stephen were trying hard to read the other person's writing. They were trying to take turns. Brian and Daniel were talking about the rest of Daniel's story because he didn't have that much of it written yet and so Brian helped A LOT! Lilly and Marcela were making Marcela's writing easier to understand by stopping every time her writing didn't make sense and fixing what was confusing. Such amazing partnerships! I *knew* all of you were ready for this!"

When any of us try something new, we aren't particularly skilled yet. Your children will not be proficient partners for each other. But now is not the time to zero in on little issues. Now is the time to help children become invested in the important work of being partners for each other.

When Natalie and I watched partners, we saw that Shawn and Stephen were simultaneously reading their own writing aloud to the other person. Neither even looked at the other's writing. Brian and Daniel were stuck because Daniel had not written very much, and it looked like Brian didn't know what to say about Daniel's skimpy text. Nicole and Juliser were sure that school was not spelled c-h-o-w-o-l, but they weren't getting in there to make the changes. [*Fig. X-1*]

Lilly told Marcela that her writing did not make sense, but Lilly couldn't say exactly what was wrong about it. These were the first things Natalie and I saw when we observed the partnerships.

But then we tried to look with new eyes and this time we also saw, floating above these less-than-perfect partnerships, that no one punched each other, that every partnership tried hard to do some good work, and that even when they got stuck, the partners stayed quiet and stayed together.

The point is that we need to believe in the power of positive thinking, and to role-play our kids into being the kinds of people who can do this work. Now is the time to lavish this new arrangement with support, trusting that a certain number of the issues will just go away. The ones that linger can be addressed in good time.

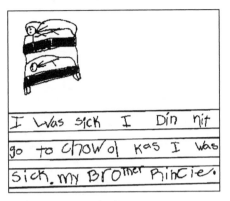

Fig. X-1   Nicole and Juliser

I was sick.
I didn't go to school
'cause I was sick.
My brother Richie [was too].

REVISING WITH PARTNERS

GETTING READY

- Text of your writing on a chart booklet.
- Children sitting with their new reading partnerships. Be sure one child recalls that he or she is partner one, and other, partner two.
- Children holding their writing folders with last session's piece still in it. That is, stop the temporary procedure of giving kids a new piece each day. Let them continue on with an existing piece.
- See CD-ROM for resources

YOU'LL LEAD THE BRIEFEST POSSIBLE MINILESSON *at the start of writing time in this session. It will simply remind writers to reread both to edit and to plan their next bit of text. You'll send off writers who are filled with resolve to write a lot.*

Your longer minilesson will be directly before the partnership share. Your goal in that minilesson will be to nudge partners to reread to check for missing words.

You may ask, why do missing words merit such attention—does it happen so often? The truth is that this minilesson is designed with an ulterior motive in mind. By asking children to scrutinize their texts to be sure there isn't a single missing word, your children will examine each other's texts paying close attention to both meaning and print. You will also be teaching your kids that when writing doesn't make sense, a reader/writer asks, "What's the problem?" then finds a clear, obvious way to improve the text. In these ways, then, this minilesson will reinforce your children's awareness that writing needs to make sense, and when it doesn't, it can often be fixed.

In this session, you teach a tiny minilesson at the start of the workshop designed to rally writers to write a lot and to write for readers. In a longer minilesson just before a partnership share at the end of the workshop, you teach partners to reread each other's writing closely looking for missing words and fixing matters.

THE MINILESSON

Connection

Tell children that you'll teach them how (and why) to reread their own writing.

"You'll see I've given you back yesterday's writing. I know some of you didn't quite finish it and you'll want to add on to it. Before you continue writing, you'll want to reread. Whenever I sit down to write, I always begin by rereading what I've written so far. The good news is that when we take extra care to write so *others* can read our writing, then we can read our writing too. Usually, I reread my writing twice, and today I'll show you how I do that."

Teaching

Show children how you reread with pen in hand, fixing little things.

"First, I reread very carefully with my pen in hand, checking that everything is okay and fixing little things that aren't okay. So watch.

I reread.

"'I lost 3 sacks' Oh! *Socks*!" I correct it. "'the wash.' Oops, I left out *in*" I insert it. "'I found 2 inside leg of' Oops. I left out *the*." I insert it. "'mi pants.' Oh! It's *my*."

"I hope all of you do what I've done and reread with your pen in hand, making small corrections."

You'll recall that lately you've been allotting each child a new booklet every day. The purpose was only to light a fire under them and get them producing more. This session's minilesson requires that you allow them to work across days on a piece.

You may ask whether this editing work shouldn't be postponed until the piece is finished and it is true that generally, we encourage writers to draft and make content revisions without a great concern for correctness, postponing editing until just prior to publication. But for young children, an attention to spelling can't come last. To get anything on the page, they need to attend to spelling. And the quick little corrections they make while rereading allow the piece to reach readers. The goal, now, isn't perfection or correctness. It's just to bring the piece up a notch.

Now show children how you reread to determine what you'll say next.

"Then I reread again, this time to get a running start on what I want to say next. This time I read and when the words run out, I say what I wish I will write next.

"'I lost 3 socks in the wash. I found 2 inside the leg of my pants. *'The other one is gone for good.'*

"Now I start writing what I said, 'The other one. . . .'"

Active Engagement

Ask children to tell their partners the two ways they'll reread today.

"Today, before you write, would you reread, and do this in two ways. Tell your partner the two ways you'll read."

Link

Rally your kids to reread and then to write for readers.

"Thumbs up if you are ready to reread, and then to write so people can read your writing. You'll share your writing with your partner at the end of today's workshop, so write so your partner can read what you say. Okay. Off you go."

SECOND MINILESSON

Connection

Remind children that earlier today, they were working with a partner to make their writing easier to read. Now you will show them how partners can help notice when they have left out a word.

"Alright everyone, during yesterday's share, you did a great job sharing your stories with a partner. I know your partners took care of your feelings. Today your partner will continue to make you feel great as a writer, but your partner will also help you make your writing easier to read. And I want to show you one particular way partners can help each other."

You probably reread your own writing in just these ways but do not stop to notice that you do this. Try to watch your own strategies as a reader and a writer because your awareness of what you do can provide you with an endless source of content to teach.

If you are being a discerning reader, you will have noticed that in this unit of study, once we have taught children a strategy in the minilesson, we are quite likely to insist they all use that strategy today. In most of our units, we're apt to say, "So add this strategy to your repertoire and when you come to a time or place where it'll help, use it." The difference is that a strategy like rereading one's work to get momentum for what we'll say next is something writers do often and every day. Requiring that all children do this strategy today doesn't take away a child's right to plan his or her topic and to write with independence.

Remember that your minilesson at the start of today's workshop was a tiny one so that you could teach your major point now, just prior to when partners convene.

Teaching

Tell the children that sometimes writers think so hard and write so fast that we forget to write every little word we need. The good news is that by reading our writing, writing partners help us find and fix missing words.

"Writers, when writers try really hard to get the whole story we want to tell onto the paper, in our hurry we sometimes forget to write all of the words we need. The good news is that a writing partner can really help us with this. I'll show you."

"Start with partner two's story today. Put it between you like you put books between you during reading workshop."

Demonstrate with one child. Show that you and your partner both read, using your fingers to follow words. When you (the reader) say something the writer didn't intend to say, or when you can't read anything, stop and work together to fix what is wrong.

"Okay, writers, I have Marcela sitting up here next to me so that we can be partners. Watch what we do so you can do similar things with your partner. Notice that Marcela's story is in between us just like books are between us in the reading workshop. And first, we look at the book and think about it." Turning to role play, she said, "Marcela, I see you wrote about you in bed."

"Yeah, on Sunday morning. I watch TV all day."

"On this page, you get up."

"Yeah, at lunch time, I have breakfast."

"This is Marcela's story, so she is the writer and I am the reader. I'll try to read it. Marcela will listen carefully to make sure that I say what she wanted to say. If I say something she doesn't want in her story or if I can't read it, she'll fix it."

"Now I'll read and we'll both point."

"When you read writing, it helps if you both point under each word." (She showed what she meant by putting her hand along side her partner's so they both pointed to the same spot.)

Natalie read in this way with Marcela and they found a missing word.

This is a beautiful way to describe how it is that writers sometimes leave out words by mistake when they write.

When Natalie asks children to put one child's writing between two partners as they do during reading time, Natalie is telling her children to sit hip-to-hip with one copy of the text held between the two of them.

Notice that instead of talking on and on about effective partnerships, Natalie demonstrates.

Our children's writing gives us glimpses into their lives.

In this minilesson, children watched Natalie and Marcela sit alongside each other and work in general ways as partners. But the viewers can't see their hands on the print enough to understand the fine points. Another way to do this would have been to read a text on an overhead projector, in which case, viewers could follow the details of the readers' work with texts.

"When something doesn't make sense, you both need to stop and do something. You might find the problem is a missing word so you'll need to add it."

Marcela added the word that she and Natalie had found was missing. "You see how we fixed what was wrong?"

Active Engagement

Ask them to read one partner's writing, looking especially for missing words.

"Writers, would you take out partner two's writing. For now, while we're on the carpet, we'll just read the first page or so of our partner's writing. Sit close with your partners. Remember, first the writer—partner two—talks about the picture and then, you point together while *the reader*—partner one—tries to read it. If there is trouble, work together to fix up the piece." They did this.

Link

Tell children that today and every day when they work with their partners, they should work just like this, fingers pointing together, the reader trying to read, the writer listening and watching.

"Okay writers, today and every day when you work with your writing partners, I want you to work like this. Both of you will point to the words. The writer will listen and watch, the reader will read. Readers, only ask for help from the writer after you try, try, try, and decide you can't continue. And writers, if the reader needs you to rescue your writing, then you will want to fix whatever gave the reader trouble."

"Who feels ready to try this work? Those of you who raised your hands can go to partner two's writing spot (that can be your meeting space) and get started reading partner two's writing. If any of you need some help, gather round closer and we'll talk."

The reason that we say, "Read partner two's writing . . ." is that children waste a lot of time deciding who will do what. We don't have time to spare in a minilesson. The reason children only read the first page of one child's writing is that we carefully curtail minilessons so they don't last longer than ten minutes.

It will seem odd for the reader to be the one to read the text. You will have to reinforce this.

Usually, we don't send children off from the meeting area when they do partner work but this minilesson is at the end of the workshop, and the partnership work may last longer than usual.

Time to Confer

Each unit of study puts new demands on your ability to confer. This unit especially should have taught you to give children guided practice in hearing and recording sounds, using high frequency words, rereading in the midst of writing, and leaving spaces between words. With any luck, you will have learned to get children started doing what you hope they'll do, and to interject lean, efficient prompts that lift the level of what they're doing. It's worthwhile to tape record yourself and to listen again to your teaching. Do you give children the time they need to be active and to encounter and solve their own problems? It is very easy to butt in too quickly, cutting children off. Do you decide what you will teach, and choose wisely enough that your children are soon able to do alone whatever they did first with your support? You can judge your conference by whether you are enabling children to do more and especially to do more even when you are no longer with them. See "Say and Record a Word, Then Reread," "Let Me Help You Put Some Words Down," and "Reread as You Write, Paying Attention to White Spaces and Spelling."

This conference in *The Conferring Handbook* may be especially helpful today:

▶ *"Say and Record a Word, Then Reread"*

Also, if you have *Conferring with Primary Writers*, you may want to refer to the following conferences:

▶ "Let Me Help You Put Some Words Down"
▶ "Reread as you Write, Paying Attention to White Spaces and Spelling"

AFTER-THE-WORKSHOP SHARE

Ask the children to find a book that can teach them how to make their writing easier to read. Ask them to take what they learn from looking at the book and apply it.

"Writers, I've shown you lots of ways that you can make your writing more readable for readers. But you know what? I don't need to be your only teacher. In this room, we have a whole lot of writing teachers! Joy Cowley can teach us writing, and Bill Martin, and Eric Carle, and Mem Fox. . . ."

"Today, would you and your partner get a book you love, one you know well, and look at what that author did to make his or her writing easy to read. Put your writing beside the book and talk about what your author did that you could try. See if each of you can find your own tip on how to make your writing better for readers. Okay? Partners on this side of the room, I'm going to give you till the count of ten only to find a book you want to learn from. Okay, the rest of you, find a book *you* want to learn from."

So far, this unit of study has lacked some of the razzle-dazzle of other units. You've kept your children's focus on very fundamental, print-based aspects of writing. This share session allows children to spread their wings a bit. Meanwhile, the truth is that every convention they could learn to incorporate will be right there in the children's literature they love most, ready to be evaluated.

You will want to look at your students' writing often, and to deliberately select the lens with which you'll view the writing. You'll find it fascinating to look at your whole class in terms of any of these things:

- Word endings
- Literary language
- Sentence structure
- Variety of punctuation
- Volume of writing
- Spellings for familiar chunks (ly, tion, ing, le)
- Vowels
- Penmanship. Is the writer making letters top to bottom?
- Evidence of editing and revision

As you look with any one of these lenses, loosely categorize your children, letting the categories emerge from what you see. Consider teaching children in one category small group strategy lessons.

For example, I could gather the four children whose work is shown and teach them to stop mixing upper case letters with lower case letters. The children represent a wide variety in ability level, and yet my grouping of these children would be needs-based. In a small group work, I could ask these children to select one sentence from their story and rewrite it without mixing lower and upper case letters. Then, I would ask each to start a new story in front of me and I would watch for and coach into consistent use of lower and upper case letters.

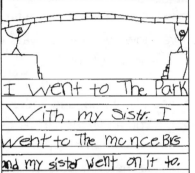

I went to the park with my sister. I went to the monkey bars and my sister went on it too.

I saw flowers and I saw my uncle. They were red flowers.

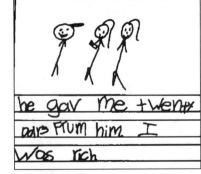

He gave me twenty dollars from him. I was rich.

Fig. XI-1 Omar

I danced with my friends.

We stopped dancing.

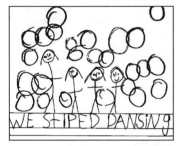

Sidney Ana played.

Fig. XI-2 Mary

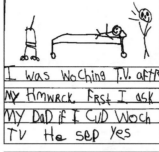

I was watching T.V. after my homework. First I ask my dad if I could watch T.V. He said, "Yes."

Then my dad called me for dinner. So I went to eat my food.

After dinner I went back to my room and watched T.V. again.

Fig. XI-3 Ravi

I was playing hockey ball in my house.

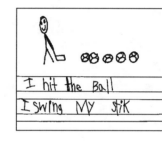

I hit the ball. I swing my stick.

It hit the wall. Boom!

Fig. XI-4 Ben

PEER-EDITING: ADDING MORE SOUNDS

GETTING READY

- Sample sentence to fix, written on chart paper
- Two-syllable word to fix, written on chart paper, with only one letter for each syllable
- See CD-ROM for resources

THE LAST SESSION'S MINILESSON ENCOURAGED PARTNERS *to look for missing words in each other's work. The goal of that minilesson was not only that partners check for missing words, but also that the reader learn to work closely, doggedly, with the exact text, reading what was actually on the page in a way that revealed problems. Close reading popped out issues, including the fact that some writers had left out words and sometimes spelled in ways no one could decipher.*

In this session, you'll try to turn your children's inevitable struggles to read each others' invented spellings into constructive work on spelling. This won't be easy. Normally, if a reader encounters the word black *spelled* bak, *the writer will simply say, "That's supposed to say 'It's black,'" and the two children will continue merrily on their way down the trail of print.*

One way to help writers turn close reading into constructive work on spelling is for the reader to correct the word, saying, for example, "You need to add an l." *But your goal is for writers to learn to write more readable texts on their own. The goal is to lift the level of what writers do another day with another piece. The strategy of turning readers into peer-editors doesn't necessarily have a lot of transference. Instead, you'll teach readers to nudge writers to include more letters in a word, making their writing easier to read. You are hoping that the partnerships put pressure on writers to provide more complete spellings.*

THE MINILESSON

Connection

Remind writers to use all they know to write readable writing.

"Writers, we'll save our longer minilesson until just before our partner share. For now, let me just remind you to use everything you know today to make your story a good one."

Teaching and Active Engagement

Ask writers to recall strategies with their partners that will help them write readable writing.

"Let's count on our fingers five things we know that can help us write great stories that our friends can read. You and your partner, talk together and see what you come up with."

Natalie and I eavesdropped as children listed strategies to each other. Convening the class, Natalie said,

"I heard you say:

▸ We need to reread our stories first, and do this with our pointer fingers checking for leftover words.

▸ We need to remember, if we come to a word-wall word, to take that extra second to spell it right.

▸ If we can't remember how to spell a word on the word wall, we can look at the word, notice it, take a picture in our mind, then look away and try to spell it.

▸ If we come to a hard word, we need to say it slowly, listen for a sound, write that sound down, then reread what we've written and say more.

▸ We need to remember to write with details."

Remember, the real minilesson comes at the end of this workshop again.

This is great practice for our children who are later writing non-narrative texts in which they are trying to teach someone else how to do something. There are two main structures in written language: stories and lists. Early in the year, children practice storytelling by sharing small vignettes from their lives, both orally and in the writing workshop. Meanwhile, however, it is also valuable for them to learn to collect parallel items and to tell them in a list.

It probably isn't true that you overheard such an informed list, but you can pretend that you did.

Link

Send children off, reminding them there will be another minilesson before the partnership time.

"That's a lot to remember! I'll be admiring you as you work—and we'll have another minilesson just before our partnerships. Remember to write in such a way that your partner will have no trouble reading your writing."

SECOND MINILESSON

Connection

Remind children that in the last session, they found words missing from their writing. Tell them that today they may find they need to write more sounds for words.

"Writers, remember that in our last workshop we read carefully and found that often when our writing didn't make sense, our pieces turned out to have missing words! I think you already know that *sometimes* when our reader can't reread, the trouble is that we need to add more letters to words that are hard to spell. We need to give ourselves a second chance at those hard-to-spell words. Today we'll learn that if we really listen to a hard word, we can often add more letters—and this will make our stories easier to read."

Teaching

Tell children how to work with their partners to write more letters per word.

"Folks, in a few minutes, you will again read your work with your partner. You will sit side by side, like Alain and I. Both the *writer* (that's me) and the *reader* (that's Alain), need to look closely at the writing. When we come to a word that Alain can't read, he will hand my paper back. Then I'll cross out the first spelling and move to the space above that word and try again to spell it. Alain will help me listen carefully. We'll both say the word a few times. Then I will try to write a letter for each sound I hear. If my partner sees that I'm not writing a letter for a sound, he will say the word again and see if I can write a letter for the missing sound. (He isn't just going *to tell me* how to spell a word!) So watch," Natalie said, and she and Alain reenacted what Natalie had just described.

Once you send children off to work, you might want to hold to what you said and spend the first ten minutes of the workshop simply admiring what they can do, recording what you see on your conferring record sheet. It is important to refrain from conferring sometimes so you can focus on observations.

There are emotional overtones to the words we use to describe the writing process. How nice to refer to correcting one's errors as "getting a second chance."

When it is time to teach, you can do so using one of four possible methods—the same four methods that you also use in conferences. In this unit of study, Natalie usually teaches using the method of demonstration. Notice that she doesn't write a novel in front of her children. She doesn't dazzle her children with displays of her superior skills. Instead, she shows her children what it is she hopes they will all do soon. Here she first explains and only later demonstrates.

Ask partners to read the word as the writer spelled it to make missing letters obvious.

"When I think I have spelled the word as best I can, my partner reads *the word the way I wrote it*. Sometimes when the reader does this, I notice some letters are still missing, and try harder."

Active Engagement

Ask the children to be your partner on a word that you need to fix.

"So writers, I have some of my writing here. I want *all* of you, not just Alain, to be my partner now. Try to read it. If I have any words that are hard to read, pass the paper back to me, okay." The children started to read Natalie's sentence.

My brothr tok me to the cs.

"What is that last word?" Brian asked.

"Circus."

"You need more letters to make it say *circus*."

"You gotta write it again on top," Samantha said.

"So how do I write it?" Natalie asked her children. "What should I write? Tell me what letters to write." Then, in a stage whisper, she said, "Truly, everyone, you gotta make *me* do it!"

"You gotta sound it out," Alain said.

"You mean I got to say it and listen to the sounds? Aww. . . . Okay. Circus, circus, circus." Natalie said, looking hard at the letters she'd written (cs).

"You gotta add more."

"You know, you're right. I think I have the right letter for the beginning and the ending, but I need more letters in the middle. Circus. Ci /r/. I hear an /r/. (She inserted an *r*.) Let me reread what I have so far, that's what I'll do." Putting her finger under the first letter and moving to the r, she said, 'Cir . . . cus, cus, /k/ /u/ /s/' I need a c and a u like umbrella. Then an s at the end."

This will provide the reader with lots of good practice and it will be great fun—unless it's done in ways that make the writer feel bad. Watch for this.

Whenever you step into the role of a child, the children know that, of course, you are role-playing. So be a little bit of a ham and let them have some fun. Beg for them to just tell you the letters to write so you can shift into the teacher-coaching role and whisper, "Make me do it myself!"

Don't belabor this. This is not the time to actually teach sound-letter correspondence so don't let the details dwarf the point of the lesson. The point is that partners have a role to play in helping writers reread and edit.

"Can someone read me what I've written?"

Stephen read, "My brother took me to the circus."

Link

Tell the children that when they work with their partners today, you want them to work just like they did with you.

"When you work with your writing friend today, and every day, if you come to a word that needs more letters, help each other just like you helped me. You can spell words better if you work together."

The work these children are doing is essential not only to writing but also to reading. As writers and as readers, they need to shift between the narrowed-in work with letters and sounds, and then the sentence-level work. The ability to shift back and forth between attending to the whole thing and attending to the little parts is crucial not only to writing but also to reading.

You'll want to circle among the partners, checking on what they are doing. Be on the lookout for partners who are fixing words for the writer rather than nudging the writer to hear more sounds and write more letters.

In every classroom, there are a few children whose growth curve will be of concern. You'll probably find that the children who struggle as writers also struggle as readers. As soon as you see signs that some children need extra help, supply that help. Make a special point of forcing yourself to notice what your struggling writers do independently when they write. Tell yourself that just as you do hands-off observations (without rescuing) when you take running records of your readers, so, too, you need to stop scaffolding your writers enough to take in what they can and can't do as writers. For each struggler, decide on a few next steps. Your goal isn't perfect spelling or spacing—your goal is for each child to begin to make steady progress. Be sure you coach these kids, then pull back and let them do whatever it is you are trying to teach on their own. Now watch without intervening, then intervene to coach and then again pull back to watch. Your goal has to be independence, even if the children are operating at a very basic level.

 These conferences in *The Conferring Handbook* may be especially helpful today:

▶ *"Say and Record a Word, Then Reread"*
▶ *"If You Erase That Word and Scoot It Over, It Will Be Easier to Read"*
▶ *"Famous Writers Use Periods to Tell Readers Where to Stop"*

Also, if you have *Conferring with Primary Writers*, you may want to refer to the conferences in part three.

After-the-Workshop Share

Spotlight an effective partnership. Write one writer's text on chart paper and ask his reader-partner to demonstrate how he helps the writer.

To spotlight Manny and Daniel's partnership, Natalie wrote one of Daniel's sentences up on a piece of chart paper. Then she had the partners replay the way they'd worked together. Natalie began by saying, "This is a sentence from Daniel's writing. Watch Manny and notice what a good partner he is!"

Manny read the sentence, "My sr (?) went to the prk." Then, pointing to *sr*, he said, "I don't know what that word is."

Daniel said, "It's sister."

Manny passed Daniel the marker. Daniel crossed out the existing spelling and moved his hand close to the space. Then he said, "Sister, *sister*," and looked at Manny as if for help. Manny joined him in saying the word again, more slowly. Then Daniel said, "I hear an s and an r at the end, but I don't hear no middle part."

Manny put his finger under the s and he read /sss/ and then made a short *i* sound. Daniel's face lit up, and he wrote *si* above the original effort.

"Do it again," Natalie said, and again Manny put his finger back to the beginning of the word. This time Daniel read, "si" and made an /s/ sound and again his face lit up and he wrote another s. On his own now, he put his finger back to the beginning of the word. He reads *sis* - and made a /t/ sound. He added a t and read, "Sist" and made an /r/ sound. He put an r on the end of the word and read, "Sister."

Daniel passed the writing to Manny who read, "Sister."

Remind children that you hope they all are being good partners.

"Great work partners! Did you see the way Manny was paying attention to what Daniel was doing? He didn't take the job away from Daniel, did he? I hope we can all be partners like these two are."

In this unit, much of your instruction highlights the interation between a child and the print he has written. You will often need to produce enlarged texts of children's work to spotlight the print work of their writing. It won't take you more than a minute or two to copy one sentence from a child's booklet, and one sentence is usually all you'll need.

This description of Daniel's effort to write one word may not be fascinating to read. But this slow, incremented process of saying a word, isolating and recording a sound, rereading, and saying what remains to be written, is the process writers need to use until they learn to spell chunks (at which time, Daniel will hear /is/ and write that chunk). If a child doesn't proceed in this fashion and instead says the whole word, writes some letters, then, without reading, says the whole word again and again writes some more letters, then the result can be havoc.

Natalie and I felt like it was again time to take a look at the whole class's writing. We knew that in a few more days, we would be celebrating their writing. This time we looked at their writing with our goals by our side, and as we noticed what each child could and could not do, we made notes about what we had and had not managed to teach. We wanted to figure out what we still needed to teach before we finished this unit. As Natalie and I looked at their writing, we thought, "What can we teach our writers that they seem just about ready to do? What will help them the most in our upcoming unit?" Because we would be working on revision next, we wanted to teach a strategy that we knew these children would practice again while revising their writing.

We decided to return to the importance of spelling high frequency words correctly. We had already told children that they needed to use the word wall to help them spell those words correctly and easily. But saying this on a few occasions isn't enough. One way to reinforce the importance of the word wall might be to use partners to help children remember to use word-wall words in their writing. We also decided to remind (and teach) writers to use end punctuation. This had been less of an issue with Natalie's children at the start of the unit because at that time, they tended then to write one sentence per page. Now, because they were pushing themselves to write more on every page, it was becoming crucial for them to learn to separate their thoughts.

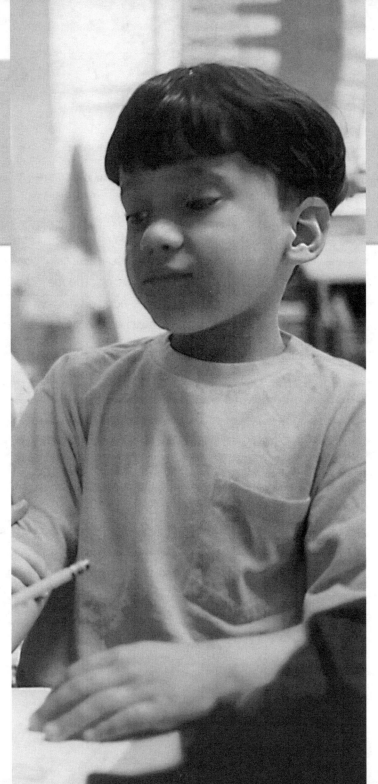

PEER-EDITING: SPELLING

GETTING READY

▸ Writing folders and personal word walls with children on rug

◉ See CD-ROM for resources

IT IS TREMENDOUSLY IMPORTANT *for your children's growth as readers and as writers that they develop a repertoire of words they know with automaticity and that they make maximum use of those as they write and read. Before you leave this unit, then, you'll want to make sure children know and use word-wall words. One way to do this is to build social support for using the word walls.*

You may want to suggest that partnerships meet at the start and finish of the writing workshop today, and that both times, they remember to check for missing words, help each other hear sounds, and, above all, keep an eye out for the words they know in a snap.

If partners help writers check that they've written their word-wall words correctly, this will create the conversations that remind writers to take the time to spell familiar words correctly.

THE MINILESSON

Connection

Tell students that today they are going to make sure that they are spelling word-wall words correctly when they write.

"Partners, you've been great at helping writers listen to words and record letters that matched sounds. Today it's still important for partners to help writers with words. This time, partners, will you help make sure your writer has spelled word-wall words correctly? Writers often have someone—we call the person an editor—who helps us check that we spell so people know what we're saying. Before we give our writing to an editor/checker, we edit—or check—it ourselves. I'll show you how."

Teaching

Teach children to be word-wall detectives, searching their partner's writing for words that are on the word wall and circling those that are not spelled correctly.

"Writers, I want to show you how I make sure I spell word-wall words correctly. Remember how Sebastien taught us to reread our word walls? Sometimes I do that, just to remind myself of the words I should know in a snap. Would you help me read the word wall now?" We read it in unison, with my pointer under the words.

"Then I sometimes reread my writing to be sure I have spelled my word-wall words correctly. Watch how I do that," I said. "I'm going to be a word-wall detective." I began to read my draft, touching each word (as if asking, "Is this a word-wall word?") "When I come to a word-wall word and notice that it doesn't seem right (which I did for a few but not all of my misspelled word-wall words), I circle it."

At Mary's (hose) we had ic krem with wip krem.
(Mi)c krem had nuts.
I pretnded it waz a weding cake.

I've brought the minilesson back to its normal spot at the start of a writing workshop. Notice the way I try to generalize today's lesson so that instead of simply assigning writers and their partners to attend to high-frequency words, I remind children that writers do this often when they write. As much as possible, it is important to teach not only towards today, but also towards everyday.

"Now I'm going to fix those words," I said, and beside *mi*, I wrote *my*. For *hose* I said, "I can't remember how to spell *house*," and looked at the word on the wall. I muttered, "Oh, yes, I see *ou* like in *out*. I've got it now," and looked away from the word on the wall and fixed my spelling.

"Be sure that you study the word-wall word, noticing its features. Then you almost take a mental snapshot of it. Only after this do you look away and try to write it without copying it. Finally, you double-check what you've done."

Active Engagement

Tell writers they are going to be word-wall word detectives to find misspelled word-wall words.

"Now I'm going to bring my writing to my partner (would you all be my partner?) What you need to do is to read my writing with me and see if *you* can be word-wall word detectives. See if I missed any word-wall words that aren't spelled right. Would you read it over to yourself and let me know what you think?" They did this, then hands flew up.

"You forgot *was*: w-a-s."

"Oh, you're right! Thanks so much," I said and corrected the word.

Link

Remind students that as writers they should be their own word-wall detectives, noticing their words and fixing them.

"Don't wait until your partner reads your writing and tells you you've got incorrect word-wall words. Try to spell those words correctly on your own. Remember that your job is to write word-wall words so correctly that you have almost no circles on your page. But of course, you'll also want to rush and get your story down and it's okay to hurry and to need to come back to check words. Later, there'll be time for you to edit, for you to double-check, and then partners will help each other too."

When you do a demonstration such as this, slow down. Look at mi, visibly let yourself think, "How is my spelled?" Say the word to yourself. As you do all this, your children will be doing this work with you. You want them to beat you to your conclusion so that your demonstration gives them practice. Don't call for their participation and orchestrate it, but know that if you proceed slowly and let them see each step as you do it, they'll be with you. Circle my and then visibly eyeball it, showing that you look and think, "Yeah, that looks right."

Give children a moment to actually do it. Don't just call on the very first hand that goes up. Let them all have a chance to practice this checking sort of a reading.

It's nice to give children the very concrete goal of writing in such a way that "they have almost no circles on the page."

TIME TO CONFER

You'll want to be sure to confer with your checklist in hand and to take careful note of what children can do, of what they can almost do, and what they can't come close to doing. As you fill in the chart, if you see something that you want to teach to five or six writers—pull them together for a strategy lesson. If you see other things that half the class needs—you've got yourself a great topic for a minilesson.

Remember to pay attention not only to what children show you on their papers, but also to what you notice by watching their processes. For example, if you watch children as they work, you might notice that some children take several breaks midway through each sentence. These same children might produce sentences that are discombobulated. You might want to teach writers that it's best to take a break only at the end of a page. You might notice that some children only reread the word they've just written or the sentence. These same children might not produce cohesive texts with unified tenses. You won't be able to teach first graders about past, present, and future tenses, but you will certainly want to teach children to reread their whole stories, putting the pages together and listening for whether the whole story "sounds right."

 These conferences in *The Conferring Handbook* may be especially helpful today:

- "Say and Record a Word, Then Reread"
- "If You Erase That Word and Scoot It Over, It Will Be Easier to Read"
- "Famous Writers Use Periods to Tell Readers Where to Stop"

Also, if you have *Conferring with Primary Writers*, you may want to refer to the conferences in part three.

AFTER-THE-WORKSHOP SHARE

Ask children to check for words they may have misspelled. After they circle possible mistakes, ask them to work with a partner to correct the spellings.

"Writers, it's time to stop writing. Would each of you take a few minutes to edit your writing? Reread it with your pen in hand asking, 'Did I spell the words I almost know correctly?' and if you aren't sure, circle a word and then later you can find it on the word wall (or somewhere else in the room), study it, and then fix it up. I'll give you a few minutes to do this, then we'll get with our partners." They did.

"Writers, would partners exchange writing? Read each other's pieces and check that your writer has spelled the word-wall words correctly. If they haven't, would you circle the word the partner missed? Then pass the story back to the writer. Give the writer a second chance with those words."

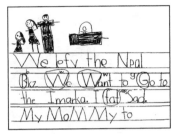

We left the Nepal because we want to go to the America.
I was sad.
My mommy too.

Plane took off.
We thinking we are coming back.

The airplane came down.
We are now in New York.
I am excited!

Fig. XIII-1   Niki

PEER-EDITING: PUNCTUATION

GETTING READY

▶ Two sentences on chart paper that do not have periods
● See CD-ROM for resources

THE LITERATURE ON PRIMARY CHILDREN'S *reading and writing development often explains that children need to develop the concept of a word. They need to learn to break speech into word units separated by spaces, and to track words amidst a page of print.*

The literature less often mentions the fact that children also need to develop the concept of a sentence. They need to understand that words are clumped together into logical units of meaning: sentences. As children begin to read and write texts that contain more words and more syntactic complexity, it is important that their minds reach for units of meaning that are larger than words.

In this minilesson, you'll encourage children to write with at least a sentence or two on each page and you'll help writers learn more about the placement of periods.

THE MINILESSON

Connection

Tell children that yesterday's work with word-wall words allows them to write faster and more—and that long stories really need periods to make them easier to read.

"Over the last few weeks, all of you have learned lots of ways to make your writing easier to read. You're stretching out your words and recording the sounds, leaving white spaces when you get to the end of a word and there are no more sounds, and you're taking the time to spell the words you almost know by heart!"

"The good news is, you're not only writing so people can read it, but you are also writing faster and more. Your writing is growing up—but you know what, now your writing is having grown-up problems. You used to write like this, 'I lov mom.' And that wasn't hard to read. Now, your stories are longer but they have a new problem."

Show the children how you have trouble reading your own writing when it doesn't have a period.

"Let me read this story to you. See if you can notice the new problem some of you are having," I said and read this:

> Today my mom and I rode bikes my bike is new when we left we rode
> beside each other then we got in a line it was fun to ride bikes it was dark
> we went home

Larry didn't require much time before he concluded, "It's got no periods so it doesn't make sense."

I nodded. "I noticed the same thing Larry. And my reading got all messed up without periods." Trying hard to read without the intonation that could rescue this piece, I read the text several times with different phrasing, as if I were totally unsure where to pause. "If I put periods, it's easier, isn't it? Now look how easy it is to read." I showed another version with correct punctuation.

"So, today, I'll teach you a bit about writing in sentences with periods."

It is not unusual for the minilessons that come toward the end of a unit to be especially targeted toward the more experienced writers in your group. There won't be time for you to ensure that every child in your class learns from a concept you teach during the final days, so you approach these lessons knowing that you are exposing your less experienced writers to a concept that you imagine your more experienced writers will be able to grasp. I expect that some of Natalie's most struggling writers will find that end punctuation is still a challenge, but I know the majority of these children will take to this instruction.

Teaching

Show children another piece of your writing and demonstrate how you reread and add punctuation.

"Sometimes when I look back over my old writing, I find a piece where I forgot punctuation. I have some of my writing here and I want you to notice how I have trouble reading it. There are no capital letters or periods so I'm not sure how to say the words. It could say:

> My sister went To a
> Circus she told me she
> Saw an
> elephant on a ball

"Or I could read it:

> My sister went
> To a circus she told
> Me she saw an elephant

"So what I do is I reread and try to read it the way I want it to go. Then I put periods in as a way to teach my reader how to read it correctly. Watch me reread and put punctuation in." I reread just, "My sister went to the circus. She told me . . ." and when I paused at the end of a sentence I said, "period," and put it in. I also switched the next letter to a capital but didn't comment on this.

Tell children that a period tells the reader to stop and think for a second before they begin the next thought.

"A period is a dot that acts as a sign to my reader. A period tells my reader how to think like I did about my story. A period is a mark that tells readers that they need to stop and think for a second about the idea they just read before they go on to the next thought."

When teaching young children, I find it really helps to put myself into their shoes and try to imagine what their experience of doing something might be. Rereading my writing in order to add end punctuation is easy for me because I find the syntactical units that comprise a text. A child who is just learning all this will probably need to try reading the text one way and another way before settling on "the right way." Children can't usually articulate their processes, so we need to observe and imagine in order to be able to teach into what children are doing.

Some teachers emphasize that periods tell the reader to pause. I'm trying to tie the period more closely to meaning than simply to pauses. But I know that either way, children won't "get it right" without repeated practice. Sometimes teachers will tell me that their children "can't even write with periods" as if this is a simple, elementary thing to do. It's not. Determining where sentences end is a complex matter. It's easier to decide between question marks, exclamation points, and periods than it is to know when a sentence ends.

Active Engagement

Ask your students to help you figure out how to use periods. First, tell your children what you want to say in your story. Then ask them to talk in pairs and finally to suggest where you should put periods.

"I need for all of you to act as my partner. Help me figure out where I need to put periods to break up the rest of my ideas. I want my story to say, 'My sister went to the circus. She told me that she saw an elephant on a ball. He walked on the very top of the ball. It kept rolling.' Let's read what I wrote and will you tell your partner where I should put periods so my words match my thinking," I said. Then I read aloud the page. "Talk to your partner."

The partners talked, and afterwards I asked for their help. Victor said, "I think you need to put the next period after *ball*."

I read the sentences with the period-pause and continued. Soon I stopped and asked, "How did that sound? Did it say what I told you I had wanted to say?" The children agreed it had. "Good. Anyone want to put a period anywhere else?"

Jana said, "And after the ball again!"

"Let me show you one more thing. Always, after you put a period, you need to make the next letter a big one. The period says one idea has ended and the capital letter tells my readers that another idea has begun."

Notice that I ask children to work this out with their partners, telling their partner what they think, rather than telling me what they think. This means that they are all active.

Link

Tell children that from now on, they need to think about using periods and capitals to separate the parts of their ideas. If they omit periods, partners can help them figure out how to separate the ideas.

"From now on, everyone, whenever you write, think about how your ideas should be broken apart. Use a period and a capital letter to let your readers know where one idea ends and another begins. These signs help readers think more like you. If you leave out periods, your partners can help you figure out where your thinking needs to be broken apart."

Although you say, "from now on . . ." you know full well that this will take children some time.

TIME TO CONFER

By this time in the unit, your kids should have lots and lots of work that they can initiate on their own. One child may be working to write with detail, another to use familiar words to help with new words, another to reread and check for sense. Be careful that you approach conferences expecting kids to have their own agendas. There are lots of equally acceptable ways they can be outgrowing themselves. Support their agendas. Let them tell you what they are working on—then teach into whatever avenue they choose.

For much of this unit, you will have tended to focus on your strugglers. This session's minilesson on end punctuation is probably most appropriate for your stronger writers.

You may want to join children in studying one page—any page—from a favorite book. "What do you notice the author has done to make us read this the way she wants us to read it?" you could ask. The child will probably point to a bit of punctuation. "So how would we have read this page if she *didn't* put that there?" you might ask. "What if she'd used (an alternative) instead?" Eventually you can ask the writer whether the author has done something the child would like to try. Skim the child's text and locate a page where the addition might make sense, and then put that page in front of the child. "So try it. Try it on this page while I watch."

These conferences in *The Conferring Handbook* may be especially helpful today:

- ▶ *"Say and Record a Word, Then Reread"*
- ▶ *"If You Erase That Word and Scoot It Over, It Will Be Easier to Read"*
- ▶ *"Famous Writers Use Periods to Tell Readers Where to Stop"*

Also, if you have *Conferring with Primary Writers,* you may want to refer to the conferences in part three.

Tell the story of a child who figured out how to use a period. Suggest that everyone can do the same.

"Writers, I'm watching your stories become much easier to read now that you are adding punctuation. On the chart paper, I've written the first page of Christopher's story. Christopher and his partner thought that he might need some punctuation to make his writing on this page easier to read and to understand. So Christopher read his writing to Sebastien, his partner, and Sebastien listened to where Christopher seemed to pause and take a breath. Listen while Christopher reads and see if you, too, can help him hear his pauses." Christopher read the line aloud, his voice showing it was two sentences. The class indicated where they thought a period needed to be inserted. "Sebastien thought the same thing," I said. "He told Christopher to put a period at the pause point, and then to start the next word with a capital letter. At first Christopher's page was written without punctuation, as if a reader was supposed to read it like this:" I read the page with no breaks. "Now the page sounds like this:" I read the page with intonation suggesting it contained two separate ideas. "Look how helpful that period is! From this day on, for the rest of your lives, each of you can put in periods that are that helpful. You just need to think about it and try hard."

SELECTING EASY-TO-READ WRITING

GETTING READY

- Children's writing folders with all of their pieces
- Construction paper to mount their stories for the celebration
- See CD-ROM for resources

IN THIS SESSION YOU WILL HELP CHILDREN PREPARE *to celebrate all of the work you have done in this unit. In the beginning of this unit, you had your writers sort through their writing folders and make two different piles. One pile was for writing that was easier to read and the other pile was for writing that was harder to read. In this session, you will ask your writers to do the same sort again. This time they will have more writing in the easier-to-read pile and they will also be more articulate about what makes writing easier to read. Once their writing is in two piles, you will have your writers share with you why they put writing in the easier-to-read pile and you will chart what they say. Then, each writer will choose one easy-to-read piece and one hard-to-read piece to share at the celebration.*

THE MINILESSON

Connection

Remind your writers that in the last session they worked on using periods to make their writing easier to read. In this session, they will be getting their writing ready for the celebration.

"Yesterday writers, you tried to make your writing easier to read by using periods to break your thinking into easier-to-understand parts. Today, you will be getting your writing ready for our end of the unit celebration."

Teaching/Active Engagement

Tell writers to go through their folders and put their writing into two piles again—an easy-to-read pile and a hard-to-read pile.

"First thing we are going to do today is go through your folders and put your writing into two piles. Do you remember how we did this at the beginning of this unit? Let's put our writing into a hard-to-read pile and an easy-to-read pile. While you are sorting today, think about *why* you are putting some of your stories in the easy-to-read pile. After you are finished, we are going to share our reasons for saying a story is easy to read."

After your writers have sorted their writing into two piles, ask them to share with the class why they called some stories easy to read. Tell them that you will write down their reasons.

"Now that you have made two piles, I want you to share some of the reasons why you put some stories in an easy-to-read pile and other stories in a hard-to-read pile. I will write down your reasons on this chart. What do you think?"

"This story is easy to read because I remembered to put spaces," Lilly said.

"I can read my writing because I put in middle letters," DiGiovanni said.

"I put ending letters on my words," said Willy.

Shawn added, "I really tried to spell some words right from the word wall."

Christopher agreed, "Yeah, and I had periods too."

This isn't a usual connection because it doesn't end with children being explicitly told what they will learn that they can use today and everyday. It's okay to sometimes have minilessons that don't fit the normal template, and it makes sense that this last day before the celebration would be such a time.

It's noteworthy to see that this unit, like many effective minilessons, is coming around full-circle. Children will revisit their earlier work, this time bringing their new knowledge and skills.

Have your writers pick one easy-to-read piece of writing for the celebration. Tell them to work with their partners to make sure the writing is as easy to read as possible. Circulate, mounting their hardest-to-read story on the top of a large sheet of construction paper, and their easiest-to-read story on the bottom.

"Writers, now that you have named some of the reasons why your writing is easy to read, I want you to pick your hardest-to-read story and your easiest-to-read story. The easy-to-read writing should be your favorite story. Once you have picked your favorite story, work with your partner to make sure that it is as easy to read as possible. We're going to publish it! While you are doing this work, I will be walking around putting your hard-to-read story on the top of a large piece of construction paper. The easy-to-read story will be put on the bottom of that same piece of paper."

Link

Remind your writers of the ways that they can make their writing easier for people to read. Remind them to use the chart to guide them as they make their stories ready for the celebration.

"Writers, as you go off to make your story ready for the celebration, I want you to remember all of the ways you can make your writing easier to read. We wrote some of those ways down on the chart. You should use these strategies to help make your stories ready for sharing at the celebration."

As you help each child mount his or her hardest-to-read piece on the top of a large sheet of construction paper and the child's easiest-to-read pieces on the bottom of the paper, you will create a before-and-after (or then-and-now) contrast. It is important for each child to feel that he or she is on a trajectory of growth because the child's past progress gives the child—and us, as teachers—reason to trust in the future.

TIME TO CONFER

In this session, you'll want to rely on the same conferences (and refer back to the conference notes you took) in Session II. This will be the perfect opportunity to assess what children have learned throughout the unit, as you have asked them to do the same task as at the beginning of the unit. Notice what children are now able to see in their own writing, notice how they talk about it, and notice the number of ways they now know they can make their writing more readable.

You will want to prepare for today by reviewing the same conferences you read in Session II: "Say and Record a Word, Then Reread," "If You Erase That Word and Scoot It Over, Then It Will Be Easier to Read," and "Reread as You Write, Paying Attention to White Space and Spelling."

Meanwhile, you may want to think about the qualities of writing you do and do not see in your children's work. Soon you and the children will be looking at their work through different lenses, asking: "Is this a focused story?" "Have I included details?" "How could I make a stronger lead? ending?" You might want to look at children's work now with an eye towards the future lessons you will teach.

These conferences in *The Conferring Handbook* may be especially helpful today:

- ▶ *"Say and Record a Word, Then Reread"*
- ▶ *"If You Erase That Word and Scoot It Over, It Will Be Easier to Read"*

Also, if you have *Conferring with Primary Writers*, you may want to refer to the following conferences:

- ▶ "Reread as You Write, Paying Attention to White Space and Spelling"

AFTER-THE-WORKSHOP SHARE

Show children some examples of the progress each of them has made and let them have some time to process it.

"Let's take a look at some of the pieces that were put on construction paper and made ready for the writing celebration." Ana chose her hardest-to-read piece [*Fig. XV-1*], and then her easiest-to-read celebration piece. [*Fig. XV-2*]

"Talk to your partner about some things you've noticed about how she has changed as a writer." They did. This is Willy's hardest-to-read writing. [*Fig. XV-3*] Willy's easiest-to-read writing is in Figure XV-4.

"Talk to your partner about some things you've noticed about how he has changed as a writer." Brian's hardest-to-read writing is in Figure XV-5. Brian's easiest-to-read writing is in Figure XV-6.

"Talk to your partner about some things you've noticed about how he has changed as a writer." Jalen's hardest-to-read writing is in Figure XV-7. Jalen's easiest-to-read writing is in Figure XV-8.

"Let's share some of the things you've noticed about all these writers!"

I heard something. It was the rain.

Fig. XV-1 Ana

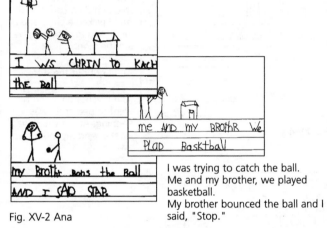

I was trying to catch the ball.
Me and my brother, we played basketball.
My brother bounced the ball and I said, "Stop."

Fig. XV-2 Ana

I was being Batman Beyond.
And I was flied.
Then I got back down.

Fig. XV-3 Willy

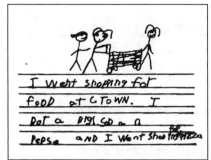

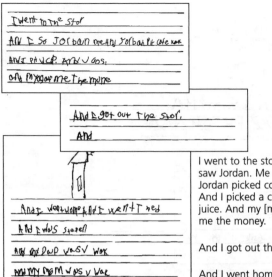

I went to the store and I saw Jordan. Me and Jordan picked coffee cake. And I picked a chips and a juice. And my [mom] gave me the money.

And I got out the store.

And I went home and I went to bed and I was sleeping. And my dad was awake. And my mom was awake.

Fig. XV-4 Willy

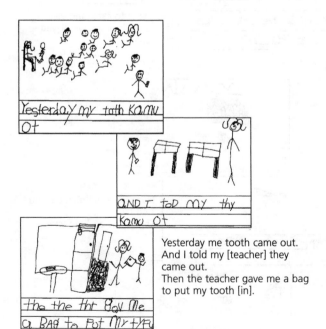

Yesterday me tooth came out. And I told my [teacher] they came out.
Then the teacher gave me a bag to put my tooth [in].

Fig. XV-5 Brian

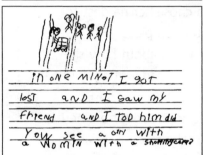

I went shopping for food at C-Town. I bought a big soda, a Pepsi, and I went shopping for pizza.

In one minute I got lost and I saw my friend. And I told him, "Did you see a girl with a woman with a shopping cart?"

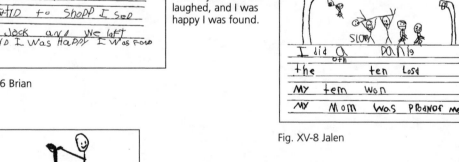

In one more minute, my mom found me. When we started to shop, I said a joke and we laughed, and I was happy I was found.

Fig. XV-6 Brian

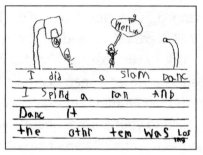

Jalen rides in the park.

Fig. XV-7 Jalen

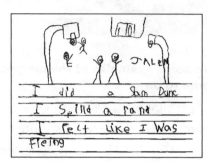

I did a slam dunk. I spinned around. I felt like I was flying.

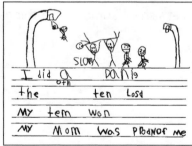

I did a slam dunk. I spinned around and dunk it. The other team was losing.

I did a slam dunk. The other team lost. My team won. My mom was proud of me.

Fig. XV-8 Jalen

SHARING AND REFLECTION: AN AUTHOR'S CELEBRATION

GETTING READY

▶ Construction-paper-mounted writing for each child
▶ Cookies and juice for guest reception
▶ Ceremonial bell
⬤ See CD-ROM for resources

IT WAS TIME FOR US TO CELEBRATE *the work we had done. For this celebration we invited some of the teachers who knew the children. We also invited some of the brothers, sisters, and cousins who were student writers at our school. Our hope was that they would benefit from this discussion about the importance of creating writing that is easy for the reader to read. You might want to invite the gym teacher, the kindergarten teachers, the reading teachers, or the second grade teachers. What is important is that you have readers in the classroom who will appreciate the work that your writers have been doing to make their stories easier to read.*

During this celebration, half of the class will be the writers sitting with their writing and the other half of the class will act as readers who visit the writers and listen to them talk about how they have changed since the beginning of this unit. Then the two halves will switch roles. The guests will participate in these discussions, giving the writers more of an audience.

THE CELEBRATION

Welcome the guests. Tell your writers that today they celebrate all of their hard work and reflect on all they've learned.

"Welcome guests, we are so happy you could come today to join our celebration! Today is the day when we celebrate all of the work we have done and all of the things we have learned over the past few weeks. All of you children are so different as writers now. When we began this work, most of you were writing stories that were hard for you to read and that were also hard for other people to read. Now, you are writing in ways that make it easy for other people to read and enjoy your stories."

Tell your writers how the celebration will proceed.

"Let me tell you how this celebration is going to work. Half of you will be authors first, and half of you will be readers first. If you are going to be an author, I will call your name and you will go with your writing to your seat. Your job will be to sit with a reader or two who will read your story. When your readers have read your story, you should tell and show them what you did to make your writing easier to read. After about ten minutes, all of you will switch roles. The author will become the readers and the readers will get a chance to share and talk about their writing. Our guests will be listening to all of you the whole time!"

Tell your children that if they find something they could do to make their stories even easier to read, do it. Give them all special-celebration, last-minute-changes pens to use in that case.

"Writers, I want to tell you one more thing before you go off to celebrate your writing. I want to tell you that as you are sharing your writing, you might find something else that you could do to make your writing even easier to read. That is good! That means that all of you are true writers. True writers know that their writing is never totally finished. If the writer decides that they want to make a change, I have special-celebration, last-minute-changes pens."

Remind your writers that today is a celebration. Remind them to congratulate each other and to enjoy each other's stories.

"Remember that today is a celebration. Let's make sure that we congratulate each other and enjoy our stories. Way to go!" The children read, listen, talk, and soak up admiration from the visitors for about twenty minutes.

Mark the moment with a ritual—in this case, ring a bell. End by reminding your writers that all of the things they have learned about writing easy-to-read stories will always be important.

"Writers, I just wanted to congratulate you again on all of the things you have learned during the past few weeks. I wanted to tell you a quick story about something that happened just now, during the celebration. Sidney and Lilly were looking at Sidney's story. When Lilly tried to read Sidney's story, she couldn't. Sidney ended up reading the story to her. After Lilly had a chance to enjoy Sidney's story she said, 'You need to put some spaces between your words so that I can read your story.' Sidney ended up getting a little mad at Lilly. But, you know what Sidney did after she got mad? She erased everything in her story and rewrote the whole thing with spaces. Can you believe it?! Just like all of you, Sidney was still pushing herself to learn more and write better, even during our writing celebration. Like all of you, Sidney is a true writer. Always working to make her ideas easier to read and understand."

"Now, I am going to give you each a chance to ring the ceremonial I-can-read-this-writing bell."

"Finally, writers I just want to say that all of the things you learned in this unit will continue to be important in our next unit. Writing in ways that are easy for other people to read will always be important because it will make it more likely that other people can understand and appreciate all of the stories you have to tell."

They each got a chance to ring the bell. As they each rang the bell, the guests broke out in spontaneous applause. Natalie and I marveled at how each child rang the bell with all of the shyness, or pride, or silliness of who they were every day in class, and yet the applause changed their faces somehow. They were proud. They knew they had worked hard, and we knew that they had been transformed as writers. They were now more in control of what they wanted to say with their writing.